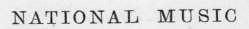

NATIONAL MUSIC

LONDON : PRINTED BY
SPOTTISWOODE AND CO., NEW-STREET SQUARE
AND PARLIAMENT STREET

THE

NATIONAL MUSIC OF

THE WORLD

BY THE LATE

HENRY FOTHERGILL CHORLEY

EDITED BY

HENRY G. HEWLETT

LONDON

SAMPSON LOW, MARSTON, SEARLE, & RIVINGTON

CROWN BUILDINGS, 188 FLEET STREET

1880

PREFACE.

THE four Lectures upon which the following Essays are based were read by the Author at the Royal Institution in 1862, and subsequently delivered at Manchester and Birmingham. Encouraged by the popular success which they achieved, and the eulogies passed upon their merits by some of his most distinguished musical contemporaries, Chorley resolved to publish them, and had partially prepared them for the press not long before his death. In the Memoir which I appended to his Autobiography and Letters* (vol. ii. p. 210), I ventured to express an opinion that they were marked in a high degree by the critic's acumen and learning, and that the

---

* Henry Fothergill Chorley: Autobiography, Memoir, and Letters. Compiled by Henry G. Hewlett. 2 vols. R. Bentley & Son, 1873.

research and speculation for which the theme afforded ample scope were supported by a profusion of illustration, attesting the wide range of Chorley's experience as a student of the art. My regret that a work so characteristic of him should remain in manuscript being shared by his legal representative, that gentleman has kindly placed it in my hands for publication.

The knowledge that in offering these essays to the world I am giving effect to the wish of my deceased friend, removes the uneasiness which one who is responsible for the publication of a posthumous work may naturally feel, lest the established reputation of its author should thereby suffer. During the eight years which have elapsed since Chorley's death I have seen no reason to believe that he has lost aught of his legitimate authority as a musical critic. By the circle which his living influence swayed, his judgment is still cited and approved. If the public taste has declared itself in favour of certain canons of art which he rejected, and one or two composers with whom he had imperfect sympathy, it has adhered in the main to the principles which he advocated, and endorsed the verdicts which he pronounced. The antagonism which his convictions and prejudices aroused is well-nigh forgotten, and full testimony has been borne by some who do not share them to his sincerity and courage. A gratifying tribute to this effect was recently rendered by the writer of a biographical sketch in Mr. Grove's ' Dictionary of Music.' The present work is happily excluded by its subject from the arena of personal controversies, and will, I trust, be equally welcomed by those who liked and disliked Chorley, as a contribution of real value to musical literature by one eminently qualified to discuss the interesting and curious points with which it deals.

The modifications which the original form of the work underwent at its author's hand have been strictly preserved, so far as it has been possible to ascertain them. These will be found in the two first essays only. The third and fourth are substantially identical with the lectures as they were delivered. Wherever the score of the selected musical illustrations was forthcoming, they have been inserted. The manuscript is occasionally obscure, but the notation has been checked by a competent musician in order to secure correctness. In a few instances the illustrations which accompanied the lectures were played either from memory or from scores that have not been retained, and these alone are perforce omitted.

H. G. H.

December 1879.

CONTENTS

———◦◊◦———

NATIONAL MUSIC OF THE WORLD.

———◦———

PRELUDE.

IT may be asserted that National Music, with its origin, its features, its uses, has been too much neglected as a subject by scientific teachers and historians, who have seemingly agreed to consider it in the light of raw material, the examination of which could only interest minute analysts or else practical manufacturers. This is a mistake. National music is *not* raw material, inasmuch as every natural production, from the moment when man has tended and shaped it, however rudely, has been thenceforth, once for all, separated from the condition of the brute ore in the mountain; or of the tree, the seeds whereof were sown by the wind, and its body dwarfed by drought or bent by storm, but from which no human hand has pruned a branch, and

B

round the roots of which the earth has never been stirred by labour.

The subject, again, has been handled ingeniously and earnestly by antiquaries who have not been professional musicians. But antiquarianism is apt, as a pursuit, to seduce the keenest and calmest of observers; and in no respect more largely than in making them partisans. I am neither scientific nor antiquarian; but the characteristics and beauties of national music have long and deeply engaged me, and its charm has found its place in my every enjoyment of the complete art; has run like a thread through my every experience of home delight and foreign travel. Thus, what I have to offer are not a few impressions, scrambled together in the haste of the moment, but are the result of many years of comparison and experience.

I conceive that the best and most profound students of the subject can offer little beyond impressions; that national music is a product to which precise test can be applied only within very restricted limits; that observation, guess, and coincidence must often be allowed to overrule tradition. Because, first, we have to take into account the uncertainty of memory, which can in no case be more largely admitted than in that of records taken down from a language varying with every untutored speaker. Every one is familiar with the game in which an anecdote, whispered along a rank of ten persons— each noting down the same as it passes—is proved to arrive at the end of its journey marvellously transformed, sometimes almost past recognition. How much more must this be the chance of melodies carried over sea and land by travellers to dwellers in lonely places; handed down by those having high, or low, or no voices, from spinning-wheel to spinning-wheel, from 'knitter in the sun to knitter in the sun,' during the ages preceding those when the manuscript recorder (supposing him competent to record) began his task. The memory has not merely to provide for tune, but for *tone* also, and without any certain appeal to musical diapason. There are memories which are organically incorrect; of this I am a living example. I have met no one with quicker and more exact retentive power than myself, and it has been in incessant exercise during thirty years; but not a few of these had elapsed before I discovered that I habitually heard every musical sound *half a note too sharp;* and this without respect to the pitch to which the instrument or the voice was tuned. It took me no small time and pains to verify this fact; and, but that it has been tested and attested again and again by others who could have no interest in maintaining a delusion, I should hesitate in offering it as testimony. I need not add, that now everything I hear passes through the process of translation.

To continue, as akin to the above speculations: the entire diapason question, in spite of the many recent attempts made to settle it, remains, and I venture to believe must long, if not for ever remain, in a most unsatisfactory state. Even if an ancient instrument is at hand to appeal to—whether it be organ pipe, or tuning fork, or bell—with the view of proving this or that fact, as regards the intonation of a musical note, it has never been established that time and climate have nothing to do with the register; that the vibrations of metal and wood are the same, after a century of wear and tear has passed, as they were at its beginning. So far from this, when, in imitation of the French commission to report on and decide the question, a similar body of men of science and skilled musicians was convened in this country, a plain truth or two came out, showing how carefully dealt with every question of the kind should be. A couple of new tuning forks had been prepared under precisely identical conditions, and with perfect agreement as to result. One was subjected to heat, and on being withdrawn from the oven was found to have changed its pitch beyond mistake. It was cooled, but it never returned to the old identity with its comrade. Thus, to be unimpeachably accurate in recollecting the tones of ill-cultivated and variable voices, or to be dogmatic in maintaining that the relic of to-day is identical with the complete instrument of by-gone ages, seem to me two impossibilities; or at least, presumptions, not warranted by reason and experience.

Another question arises, in respect to national music considered traditionally—the testimony on which we accept our knowledge of ancient instruments. This is mainly derived from monumental drawings and sculptures; which I cannot but think have been too largely accepted as literal, seeing that into every record of the kind so much of what is decorative and emblematical enters. It is true that in a certain class of objects Gothic structure may be relied on as documentary; seeing that the vine, the hawthorn, the rose, the oak leaf, the *herba benedicta* are, in its best examples, displayed with remarkable,

if formal accuracy.   When we get back to the art of
an elder world, we must allow for ideality, mysticism,
and other conventions, as modifying precise representation.   If the truth to nature of the honeysuckle
in the well-known Greek border, of the Mosaic olive-
tree selected by Mr. Ruskin in his ' Stones of Venice '
(vol. iii. p. 178), as a touching example of earnestness
and generalisation combined, be considered, we
surely find in the result a warning for more caution
than appears to have been exercised.   Who could
reason on the *genera* or habits of those flowers from
the presentments specified above ?   If we must
translate (so to say) the motionless attenuated figures
arranged in flat procession on the walls of Egyptian
tombs and temples, before we can accept them as
portraits, an analogous process may fairly be applied
to harp, pipe, and sistrum, as depicted by the primitive
sculptors and painters of old.   To the harp in
particular, as the instrument to which, beyond all
others, legendary fancy has attached itself, this
remark belongs; nor can any speculations on its
compass and capacities, as derived from the number
of strings depicted under such circumstances, be
accepted without great hesitation.

Such are some of the few uncertainties through

which tunes and traditions pass, before we arrive at another, never to be forgotten—the possible and frequent inexactness of notation. Many of the specimens of national melody we possess have been set down by persons of the slenderest possible technical acquirement, totally unable to perceive what is accidental or what is essential in this or the other chain of sounds and phrases. And who is there that will venture to vouch for the accuracy of manuscript when the same has passed into print, let the care taken to ensure correctness have been ever so exquisite? Think of the disputed readings of the Shakspeare text—think of Hayley deliberately printing Lord Bacon for Robert Cecil, Earl of Salisbury—of a modern historian setting down Sir Peregrine Pickle instead of Sir Peregrine Maitland as one of the pallbearers at the Duke of Wellington's funeral! The character in which music is noted is obviously one more tempting to inaccuracy than any verbal alphabet. We have seen in a work so modern as Beethoven's C Minor Symphony, two bars in the *scherzo* cancelled by the master's own hand, while correcting the proofs, overlooked by the printer and the public, till the fact was incontestably proved by Mendelssohn: the error in the meantime having

given rise to columns of controversy, and the blunder
having been pounced on as a rare beauty by the
transcendentalists, among them one no less ingenious
than M. Berlioz.   It is only a year or two since the
journals of Paris recorded the correction of a false F
in a work no less recent and hackneyed than the
overture to ' Guillaume Tell.'   With instances, which
could be multiplied by the thousand, such as these
—oversights arising not so much from neglect as
from imaginative quickness—few, save the wilfully
credulous, will put implicit trust in musical notation,
above all, when it is the vehicle of such crude irre-
gularities as abound in national music.

Further, we have to allow for something more
indirect in everything that concerns report of national
music.   So long as humanity shall last, the influence
of feeling no less than of fact, the circumstances of
time and place, must be taken into account, however
advanced be the state of intelligence, in all records
dealing with representative art.   Think of the raptures which have filled the pages of modern tourists,
describing as realities matters which are virtually
only so many sensations.   Two may be instanced:
the first of these being the Sistine ' *Miserere* ' in the
Holy Week at Rome.   The music of this far-famed

rite, which has enchanted so many tourists, and encouraged the birth of so many outbursts of hazy enthusiasm, if transferred from the scene of action and from under the spell of execution—as when it was surreptitiously noted down by Mozart—proves to be plain, almost to the point of prosaic simplicity, and in small degree to justify the raptures which belong either to curiosity or to the real faith and expectation attendant on the ceremony. Often as it has been described, it was not till the other day, when the letters of one partly poet, partly artist, thoroughly musician—Mendelssohn—were published, that the untravelled world had much chance of comprehending to what extent the impression made on religious and cultivated men and women was one of art, or one of scene and sympathy.

Another musical performance nearer home was, in its time, much talked of—the vesper service in the *Béguinage* at Ghent. That was still more an affair of mere framework than the Sistine 'Miserere.' The music was utterly mediocre—the voices of the sisterhood were stale or sour, and ill trained to boot. The organ, when I heard it, wheezed with decrepitude, and its keys rattled audibly. Nevertheless, the evening scene, when the demure female figures

entered silently, one by one, and each, having folded
her white kerchief on her head, dropped on her
knees, the prayer accompanied by some pretext of
musical accompaniment—was picturesque enough to
hold the recollection of those who witnessed it, and
with the majority, it appears, to confuse clear artistic
perception.

Almost the strongest impression I recollect to
have received from a tune, belongs to a Methodist
funeral, which wound its way up a hollow north-
country-lane, on a grey October afternoon. The
coffin was not caparisoned; the people who walked
before and behind it joined in a plain dry burial
psalm—sung as provincial psalm-singers used to do
forty years ago in England. It was not merely the
presence of death, which is felt so potently by the
young; but it was the unexpected, sincere intrusion
of that droning music into a still landscape, which
has printed that melody on my memory.

What has been said will apply to any part-song
of German students or vineyard girls, heard in the
stony lanes of a Rhine or Moselle or Danube village
by moonlight, after a happy day's pleasure—to any
miserable Italian opera, drunk in as so much nectar
by tourists, resolute on finding opera in Italy (espe-

cially if the same be cheap) something delicious. Crabbe says—

It is the soul that sees.

This might be fairly matched by another phrase : ' It is the sympathy that hears.'

At all events, the speculations which these outlines represent have been clearly and consistently before me, at every stage of such collection and comment as are set forth in the following essays. They approach the subject from the four points of the compass, not, however, in their established order; but from East, South, North, and West.

MUSIC FROM THE EAST.

LOOKING to the East as to the cradle of civilisation, we naturally accept every relic and record coming thence as of the very highest importance. The national music of no other countries has been so carefully studied by competent and erudite writers as this; and, if it be considered in the antiquarian and scientific point of view, the able work of Herr Engel[1] may be said in some measure to have exhausted the subject.

Viewed, however, on its picturesque side, a remark is to be offered to which, it seems to me, attention has not been sufficiently drawn. Instrumental resource was developed earlier, and with greater certainty, than any cultivation of the voice such as comes home to modern sympathies. However conventional they be, the pictures of harp and lyre (the latter the descendant of the old fabled tortoise-shell, cast on the strand, and strung with a sinew or

---

[1] *Music of the Ancient Nations.*

two)—otherwise of the instruments which are
played (the French expressively say, *pinched*) by the
fingers, or are caressed by the *plectrum* or bow—those
of pipes of every quality, whether they be blown by
the mouth, or the wind within them set in motion by
the elbow—painted on the walls of the temples and
tombs of Egypt during the times when the one were
reared behind their avenues of sphinxes, and the others
locked up in the heart of some mountainous pyramid—
have a meaning not to be misread. They indicate a
state of constancy in their fabrication; as, too, in
the ornamental luxury applied to their garniture.
Each of these must have had its own ascertained
scale, to which (for better, for worse) certain reference
could be made. There is no proof that contemporary
voices were trained to utter sounds of corresponding
precision or approach to sweetness.

My belief has long been fixed, that National
melody has never, in its beginnings, been derived
from Song so largely as from Dance—from instruments employed to accompany numbers moving in
regular figures. For in the dance, as also in the
march, there must be rhythm, and without rhythm
there can be no melody more regular than such
fitful breathings as the Æolian harp murmurs,

when some breeze provokes it to reply. A chant is not a melody. It is merely an accommodation of the speaker's voice to the words which are to be delivered by him. The words may be long or may be brief: the chanter or declaimer in music must make room for them; and the intervals of tone may, in many cases, be merely so many expedients of support and relief to the speaking voice. Every one who has frequented the exhibitions of extempore preachers must have been struck by a semi-musical delivery, which in cultivated persons approaches *tune*, which in unlettered ones is *twang*. When Edward Irving read from the Bible that splendid passage which contains the dedication anthem for the opening of Solomon's Temple, it was a spoken chorus. Elizabeth Fry sang her sermons.

The Chant, then, it is not chimerical to assume, originated unconsciously in verbal recitation. There is nothing so soon caught up, so late got rid of, as a peculiar inflexion of voice : and thus the desire of crier or speaker to be heard by those at a distance, seconded by imitation, has gone far to breed those strange barbaric sequences of sound, which have been erroneously defined as melodies.

Again : sounds independent of language grow

out of the necessities and accidents of daily labour. The English paviour solaces himself with his grunt. The mule-drivers of Spain have learned their shriek and snort among the quadrupeds they hurry forward. Out of such primitive elements as these, national chant can grow; but whenever an *instrument* is made, there must always be established something more of certainty than belongs to such vague, wandering sounds; some feeling, be it ever so imperfect, for tune, or correctness of intonation ; and, insomuch as instruments were used to inspirit or accompany the dancer, some recognition of return or periodicity—otherwise of rhythm.

The foregoing speculations have always seemed to me of great importance; almost to the point of establishing a definition and a principle. Their plausibility, at all events, can be largely proved from such specimens of Eastern music, ancient and modern, as have been collected by Villoteau, Laborde, Jomard, Sir Gore Ouseley, and that later traveller to whom art owes so much—Mr. Layard. The chants of the East, as noted by them, have one and all the same character—a certain arid melancholy—a wail which fancy cannot dissociate from the idea of coarse and languid voices, exhausted under the influence of

a fierce climate, and flung abroad into desolate space.
So long ago as the time when Kepler wrote, the close
of the sixteenth century—a time at which melody
(as we understand the word) was hardly formed,
the writer complained of the manner of singing
'which the Turks and Hungarians are accustomed
to,' as 'resembling the voices of brute animals,
rather than the sounds of the human voice.' If the
tones have become sweeter since Kepler's day (which
may be doubted), the vocal tunes, as distinguished
from dancing rhythms, have made little advance.
They are still wayward to disorderliness. Their
closes are habitually imperfect and drawn out.
These, however, are peculiarities belonging to other
wild music than that of the East. Here is a
specimen of a Priest's song, noted by Mr. Layard, [2]
which in structure, if such a word can be employed,
and in division of notes, resembles, and not distantly,
the 'Ranz des Vaches' of the Swiss.

[2] It may be as well to state, that since this specimen was
selected from among a mass of similar tunes, it has appeared in
Herr Engel's valuable volume, having probably been suggested to
him also by the extreme strength with which its characteristics are
marked. I would have withdrawn it and substituted another (to
avoid the smallest semblance of collision) were it not particularly
necessary to me in the comparison I desired to illustrate ; and did
not coincidence in selection add force to my argument.

Let us now turn to the Swiss pastoral chant.

Vivace.

The above are chants, not melodies : both of them obviously calls, intended to be heard at a distance, executed by defective voices—probably incorrectly noted—calculated to lay hold of the ear by iteration as much as by variety ; but whereas in the first chant there may be implied something of the apathy of oriental existence, in the latter fancy may hear a tone of the echo from the mountain peak ringing freshly down the valley.

When the transforming power of the apathy of the East is adverted to, one of the most curious illustrations which has turned up in these later days must not be lost sight of. This is the controversy set on foot in regard to the parentage of the tune 'Malbrouk'—a tune so insipid as not to be worth quarrelling about—a tune which may have got into the East by the agency of recent French armies : which may have come from the East in the days of the Crusaders—as persons of the time being have been bold enough to assert—but which, as the world has agreed to accept it, has such an air of Paris and of the singers belonging to Paris as no one can mistake,[3] that has ever been conversant with that delectable city, ancient or modern. Here is the tune as noted by Eastern travellers, which it will be seen is as tame, when compared with the 'Malbrouk' we are accustomed to, as if some lotos or opium eater, having got hold of a clear and easy melody, was half consciously drawling it out before dying away in his trance.

Those who paid attention to the performances of the band of the Pacha of Egypt which visited London in 1862 might, I think, detect in the midst of the strange barbaric 'jargoning,' which passed with them for harmony, fragments of Western melody imperfectly caught, and to which the impure note,

[3] It may be noted, however, among the coincidences which crowd on the collector at every step taken by him, that a curious similarity exists between the first four bars of 'Malbrouk' and those of 'Callino Casturame' arranged by William Byrd. (Chappell's *Popular Music of the Olden Time*, p. 793.) This, then, may have been one of the melodies which have grown into their present shape gradually.

once having entered, gave a semblance of character
and savagery. But I can only speak of this with
caution, since an attempt to examine the noted
music from which they played was resisted with an
unwillingness, almost amounting to such aversion as
the natives of certain countries have shown to the
magic arts of the portrait-maker.

Be the amount of vitiation what it may, be it
conceded that the tunes of certain districts of the
East may have been imported from other lands
instead of being begotten on the soil (both facts
which it is next to impossible to determine by the
most patient investigation);[4] it is certain that there
is a difference in the tunes of the East. Among
those the best noted and known, possibly because
they are the most regular, are the Hindostanee
melodies, some of which offer examples of vocal

[4] The other day, when a series of hints and instructions was
drawn out at the request of the Anthropological Society for the
guidance of collectors of national music, I ventured to suggest an
experiment which could hardly fail to be attended by some results
of interest, and might, in these, advance us a step further in our
knowledge of characteristics and their causes. Wherever the native
musicians show anything like intelligence or culture, I would have
'a test tune' (one, for instance, as universally known and easy as
'God save the King') propounded to them, with a view to their
adoption of it. From the collection of *variorum* versions which
would be gathered, certain conclusions could hardly fail to be shadowed out though it would be rash to rely on them dogmatically.

cantilena more symmetrical and civilised than those occurring in either Egypt or Arabia. Such is the air so familiar to every one, that to quote its opening phrase will suffice :

I have always conjectured that this air may have been helped by some such process as was employed by Moore to bring into form his well-known 'Canadian Boat Song,' and which converted, 'The Groves of Blarney' into the elegant melody, 'The Last Rose of Summer'—a tune which, simple as it is, consisting of two strains, one thrice repeated, has become one of European celebrity, and made the fortune of M. von Flotow's feeble opera, 'Martha.' Here is what may be the original tune, noted down at Bangalore by a competent musician, in 1854 :

If the relationship between the two last specimens be admitted, their coincidence and variation
furnish another example of that transformation of
musical phrases, among untutored singers and in-
expert players, which is never to be lost sight of by
the student of national music.

The almost universal monotony and coarseness of
the singing voices, if so they may be called, of the
Orientals, seems accompanied by inability on their
part to appreciate beauty of vocal tone in others.
This has been again and again curiously manifested
during the visits which Eastern personages of opu-
lence and cultivation have paid to Europe. When
the Persian princes were in England, some quarter
of a century since, they took small pleasure in the
opera and its singers (howbeit enchanted with the

dancing); preferring a home performance on a wretched little dulcimer by one of their own suite —as Mr. Fraser commemorated in his lively narrative—and only really captivated by the lights and the tinsel of Vauxhall, where, they said, 'true joys abounded.' I shall never forget the stolid, turmeric-coloured countenances, without a glimmer of curiosity or intelligence to light them up, with which the Japanese ambassadors witnessed one of the performances of the Sacred Harmonic Society. It might have been thought that the mass of violent sounds in the *forte* passages must have impressed them with wonderment, at least; but no, they endured the infliction in the fulness of stolidity. That was all. This insensibility to vocal charms is not necessarily a case of inexperience. It has been proved, past doubt, that a people ranking far lower in the scale of civilisation and culture than any Orientals,[5]—the North American Indians—have repeatedly expressed a passionate, ignorant delight

[5] While tracing out this incoherence, which must so perplex every one who desires to force a theory as to the connection of the fine arts, the admirable instinct (if so it be) of the Hindoos in the harmony of colours must not be overlooked. Then, apart from their mechanical perfection as specimens of inlaid metal work, the Japanese bronze vases have often a grace of form not to be exceeded by the most exquisite examples of Etruscan earthenware.

in the trained vocal music which they have found in the theatres of the great Transatlantic cities. There is something, after all, in organisation; and though it may appear presumptuous and paradoxical to venture so sweeping a definition, I must say that some research and experience have brought me to a firm belief that there are races and nations in whom certain of the finest artistic senses (capriciously enough distributed) have no existence. I dare to believe that the music of the Greeks was so much foolishness, if it be measured against their colossal drama, their divine sculpture; and nurture a secret and deep irreverence against the harpers, pipers, and symphonists, whose strange forms in the monumental sculptures of Egypt have set speculation so eagerly to work, and have beguiled so many ingenious people into conceiving that the art of music was with them something rich, complete, and attractive; the key to the cipher being untowardly lost.

The musical humour of the East seems to undergo a marked change at the points where instruments come in. At that juncture (wherever it may arrive), something distinct and precise, indicating the enjoyments of the dance or the discipline of the march, enters likewise. Here—to give an example of a

dance noted down at the 'French Rocks' in 1851,
by a competent musician- -is a tune as regular as
any devised by a French ballet composer, and, it
may be added, bearing a curious and not remote
resemblance to a style which has always been popular
in French music, and which has been carried to perfection by M. Gounod, in certain movements of his
music to 'Sappho,' 'Ulysse,' and 'Philemon and
Baucis.'

Something bolder and more vigorous is the next
specimen—a never-ending, still-beginning tune—in
great request at festivals, and which, if not helped,
as may be suspected, by notation, must rank high in
any collection of Hindoo music:—

The effect to be gained by interminable repetition can hardly be better studied than in these East Indian melodies. There is little analogous in the national music of the North, even taking in the bagpipe tunes. One more illustration of a clearly-marked characteristic may be found in the following handful of notes, which at once accompanied and incited the dancing-girls—obviously, practitioners of an inferior class—who some years ago exhibited in London:

Something not unlike this aggravating dance till

very recently walked about our London streets in
the shape of the tabret, or small drum, diligently
patted in time by a pair of ginger-bread coloured
hands, the beat of which supported and carried off
the dreary voice of the chanter. It is observable,
however, that this effect, which is rhythm in its
crudest form, has offered suggestion to composers in
search of local colour. I may instance, as a singularly felicitous example, the Temple Revel in Sir
M. Costa's 'Eli,' where the effect depends largely
on the repetition of a dull rhythmical sound, sus-
taining a dance throughout a scene of strong and
varied emotion.

In any event, this East Indian music is of homely
quality, especially considered in regard to its execution. 'The natives,' writes the friend to whom I am
indebted for three of the above specimens, 'have no
' knowledge of harmony. Their ideas go no further
' than the *nasnum* and *tom-tom*, and their souls revel
' in the delightful sounds produced by them, which are
' the horror of Europeans. At all their public festivals
' the *tom-tom* plays a principal part, these drums being
' made of hollow trees, some of the size of a good-
' sized wine-cask. I have seen them so large as to be
' placed on a waggon and drawn by oxen. The

' *nasnum* is an instrument resembling our oboe, but
' it is louder, shriller, coarser.   The bands which
' saunter about the bazaars and perform at weddings
' generally consist of two musicians, *both* playing the
' *nasnum*, the second a protracted pedal note.   The
' *tom-tom* is indispensable to all Indian music.   The
' second oboe player has often amused me by his
' power of holding out the note without any interrup-
' tion.   I have never been able to understand how.
' The first *nasnum* seems every now and then to rest
' for a few bars, whilst the second goes on *fortissimo*
' without interruption, and apparently without any
' effort.   I once observed such a player very closely,
' and found, by my watch, that he held out his note fully
' five-and-twenty minutes.   He seemed, however, to
' move his nostrils slightly and regularly, and the whole
' process did not appear to give him more trouble than
' the player has who touches the key of an organ.[6]
' Such an accomplishment would be something like a
' miracle to English players, since every one of them
' knows how difficult it is to hold out a note for
' three-quarters, or even one-half a minute.'

A large portion of that which has passed, and still

[6] This is not a surprising feat.   A chemist keeps up his blow-
pipe without intermission by his mouth, breathing meanwhile regularly through his nose.—ED.

passes, with the Chinese for music to be enjoyed, distances barbarian sympathies and defies barbarian analysis. The specimens noted by Barrow, Amiot, Du Halde, Irving, and by Herr Engel (with the one remarkable exception, of which mention has been made), are so hideously at variance with every one of our feelings, fancies, practices in art, or ideas of beauty, that one can only look at them and wonder. For wonderful it is, that a people so rich and ancient as the Chinese —one so advanced in the knowledge of secrets of colour, refinement of texture, peculiarity of form (though in beauty of the same they are obviously surpassed by the Japanese)—so skilled in exquisite caligraphy—a people, to boot, who possess a philosophy, a fiction, and a drama of their own, all indicating a separate, not an undeveloped civilisation—should appear to us, who can allow for and admire their excellences, so utterly savage and repulsive in their musical tendencies. It will not altogether fit the case, to appeal to the total absence of perspective, conventionality of outline, and flagrancy of form (often amounting to deformity), which distinguish the pictures and tissues of the country, when most refined in texture, gorgeous in material, or rich in colour. What we know of Chinese melody

and music, with very small exception, is in every
respect more rude and more shapeless than that of
far more savage peoples.   Perhaps the solution of
such an inconsistency may be found in a fact difficult
to be admitted by those who, because all the arts are
kindred, expect them to be contemporary in their
development. May we not have here a signal proof that
music has been always a vagrant Muse, with an independent and arbitrary life of her own, and that her
prosperity or the reverse can be no more predicated
from the signs and tokens of any given epoch than
can be the moods of the wind, ' which bloweth where
it listeth.'   Yet even this Chinese barbarism—(to
retort upon the Celestials with their own epithet)—is
proved by exceptions which, supposing them to be
authentic and not fabricated, are of astonishing
regularity.   In the section of Herr Engel's valuable
work on 'The Music of the Ancient Nations,' which
deals with China, is cited (p. 145), 'The Ancient
Hymn in honour of the Ancestors': a tune in the
midst of most chaotic handfuls of notes, as stately,
well ordered, and susceptible of musical treatment
as any Lutheran psalm, or any of those Romish
hymns which replaced the crude and over-prized
Ambrosian and Gregorian chants.

The solitary use of the national music of China by a trained writer which I can call to mind, is that made by Weber—of all composers, foremost and most felicitous in availing himself of what may be called *wild* music—in his overture to Schiller's translation of Carlo Gozzi's Chinese *Fiaba*—' Turandot.'

The music of the East, which I have dwelt on, is obviously too primitive and too uncouth to have been largely, if at all, recurred to as material by the trained composers of modern times, when they have been in search of what is called 'local colour.' An exception is now to be spoken of: a province (so to say), which has suggested a style, and given an inspiration to many modern artists. 'Turkish music,' —or, as they call it in Germany, Janissary music—has grown into an established musical term; as much as 'the stringed band,' and 'the wind band,' as definitions of the group of instruments which make up that magnificent machine—a modern orchestra. Yet no Oriental music seems to be so limited, and so monotonous, as the tunes which the bells, cymbals, and duller 'Turkish' instruments of percussion support, and which possibly owe their simplicity and timidity to the restricted powers of the instruments to which the melody is entrusted. A few notes of the diatonic scale have been turned to effective account,—perhaps, because their orderliness of interval and rhythm, setting them entirely apart from anything which may be called or approaches a chant, renders them amenable and available to devices of science and the desires of fancy. Here, for example, is the phrase noted by Laborde, and used twice by Weber in his 'Oberon,' first as a march on which a brilliant vocal *solo* could be embroidered:

The same phrase, with a happy touch of inversion and change of rhythm, was employed by Weber at a later period of 'Oberon' as the dance tune breathed from the horn of the Fairy King:

&c.

That such closeness of interval is a frequent, if not a constant characteristic of Turkish music, may be seen by half a score of other examples. Observe how, with the alchemy of true genius, by the use of syncopation, and of the minor mode, Mozart could turn the forms adverted to, to totally original account in the Turkish chorus of 'Die Entführung.'

Recollect again, how a later, less scrupulous, less correct, but more brilliantly gifted writer, Signor Rossini, could combine the bald vocal phrases of Turkish music and the imperious clang and thump of its instruments in the vigorous chorus from his 'Siége de Corinthe.'

Let me digress for a moment. I have not used the epithets applied to Signor Rossini, as 'a madman flings about fire,' but from a feeling which has 'grown with my growth, and strengthened with my strength'—formerly an instinct, now a deliberate conviction. I hold that since Handel, there has been no musician deserving the epithet so completely as the composer of 'Il Barbiere,' 'La Donna del Lago,' the third act of 'Otello,' the tomb-scene of 'Semiramide,' the greater portion of 'Moïse,' and 'Guillaume Tell.' One might say without strain or conceit, and with express reference to this subject of mine, that there is as much of *heather* in his Scottish opera as there is of *lagoon* in his treatment of Shakspeare's noble Venetian tragedy—of Alp and glacier and hill echoes ringing through the air, in the scenes, now fresh, now sublime, of the Swiss legend—as there is of the cruel, ceaseless, monotonous Turkish tone in the chorus of which the opening phrase has just been cited. Here is no question of science, but, to repeat, of brilliant natural gifts.

To return. The illustrations of 'Turkish Music,' and its style and capabilities, within very narrow bounds, as improved and employed by scientific musicians, could be multiplied *ad infinitum*; during as wide a range of dates as separates Andreas Romberg's 'Turkish Symphony,' written for Constantinople, from M. Felicien David's 'Desert,' which may be said to represent the quintessence of all the forms of Eastern melody with which we have been made acquainted.

Ere I have done with this sketch, I must recall another, and the most marvellous, employment of the rude and monotonous Eastern cries or tunes, in conjunction with a busy and inexorable rhythm, made by a master of his art, which stands by itself, because of its wondrous force and felicity. This is in Beethoven's chorus of the Whirling Dervishes in his 'Ruins of Athens.' The persistence in diatonic interval, which has been represented in divers forms by Mozart, Weber, Romberg, Gluck (as the airs from his 'Pilgrims of Mecca,' 'Unser dummer Pöbel meinte',[7] reminds us), and Sigr. Rossini, is by Beethoven thrown into the vocal part, while the delirious triplet accompaniment describes (if there be such a thing as description in music) the whirl of frantic feet swarming on the floor; fierce vigour and uncouth, not illicit, modulation being so wrought up as to produce the most unique, resistless specimen of mad climax which the library of music has to show. But Beethoven probably regarded the thing as a mere trifle.

I have spoken first about what may be called the ruder music of the East designedly, yet without reference to chronology. For had dates guided me, it would have been needful to begin with the music of that strange and noble people who, now having a country of their own no more, are still the earliest of those owning an oriental origin of whom distinct and consecutive record is made;—a people impossible to regard without as much fixed wonder and close

[7] Varied by Mozart (No. 455 of D. von Köchel's *Thematic Catalogue*).

study as imperfect sympathy—the three, by a somewhat ungenerous, yet not unnatural process, having too largely taken the form of antipathy which is unhappily historical. The remarkable attitude which the homeless Hebrews have maintained and retained since the birth, progress, and enlargement of Christianity even unto these days;—the supremacy they have asserted in the face of persecution, bigotry, scandal (not without some warrant to be found among the national characteristics of these people without a nation), could not fail to be accompanied by a certain injustice which, as it is the habit of injustice to do, has only fixed attention more permanently upon those who have been its object. Their place in the world of music has, from the days when, as Holy Writ informs us, Tubal Cain invented harp and organ, down to our own time, been peculiar and commanding.

From whichever side they be considered, the music of the Hebrews, and the aptitude and glory of that race for and in the art, are matters of the highest interest. Their tunes, considering the remote antiquity to which they pretend, are amazing. Though the fashions of organ, harp, lute, sackbut, psaltery, 'trumpet also, and shawm' have been

modernised, a claim attaches to some of the melodies
habitually used in the synagogues, which almost
bewilders the mind by the vast sweep which it takes
back to the early days of that peculiar people, whom
the Most High deigned to guide and protect in
their wanderings with ' a pillar of cloud by day, and
a pillar of fire by night.' Compared, I say, with
other distant echoes which have reached us from the
ancient world, the symmetry and grandeur of some
of the portions of the Hebrew Temple service—and
these reputed the oldest—are almost as remarkable
after their kind as are the Psalms of the Royal
Poet, for dignity of language and beauty of suggestion to the ' chief musicians ' and ' singers.' I
must beg, however, those who bear me company to
bear in mind also my habitual caution in dealing
with tradition—not to say, mistrust of it—even when
it is handed down to us by conscientious and learned
men.

To the work of two of these every student of
Hebrew music must be largely indebted : the un-
ambitious but carefully executed collection of ancient
melodies of the Spanish and Portuguese Hebrews, by
Mr. Edward Aguilar, with an instructive preface
by M. de Sola, the priest of the Spanish and Portu-

guese congregations in London. This furnishes
illustrations of great value, whether they be considered collaterally with reference to the music of
other countries, or singly, as standing on their own
merits. They may be divided into two sections:
the first containing those chants of a wayward
rudeness, so constant to oriental cries, and so perplexing to the ear be they ever so explicable, as
having originated in the speaker's desire to help his
voice. The following fragment,[8] though not among
the specimens reputed by M. de Sola as oldest, is
not one of the least characteristic:

Lento senza tempo.

[8] The specimen given when my lectures were delivered, was
No. 44 of M. de Sola's collection: a 'Melody of the Blessing of the
Priests,' regarding which we are assured that tradition exists that
it is identical with that sung in the Temple, where, as it was known,
the priestly choirs were daily wont to bless the people, agreeably
to the command to them in Numbers vi. 22–26. I find, however,

The manner in which this chant shifts about, opening in one tone and closing in another, is worthy of observation. I cannot but suggest, that the irregularity may be referable to imperfect transmission, caused by uncertain intonation on the part of the singer.

Many of what may be called Hebrew melodies (as distinguished from chants) bear no trace of time or place. The one I shall give has something like a universal currency, and is to be found in every collection of Hebrew music which I have been able to examine.

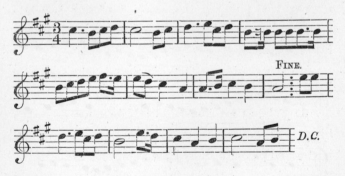

This is, surely, a grander and more tractable

that its peculiarity of character, and great reputed antiquity, have also attracted Herr Engel, who has published it in his work; and as choice was not wanting, have therefore selected an example which will be less familiar to his readers; while its preference in no respect weakens my case.

melody than Luther's well-known psalm tune, 'Ein' feste Burg,' which incited Meyerbeer—an Israelite indeed in whom there was *much* guile—to create that imperishable opera betwixt the two warring Christian faiths. And yet, what is the date of Luther's psalm tune, as compared with the age of this melody? Tradition, M. de Sola assures us, refers it to the days and deeds recorded in Exodus, when Miriam the Prophetess, the sister of Aaron, answered those who bore her company with timbrels and with dances—by her victorious chant of triumph over the destruction of Pharaoh's chariots, and all his host that pursued the children of Israel—while she sang how 'the horse and his rider were thrown into the sea.'

It must not be overlooked, that in the carefully executed preface to this excellent collection of tunes, M. de Sola, as all honest observers must do, takes his part in weakening our belief in tradition, which is strained to the utmost by the legend attached to this noble tune; for he informs us that at an early period—even as happened in other countries, where Roman Catholic masses were built upon such secular ditties as 'L'homme armé'—the custom was adopted among the Spanish and Portuguese Hebrews of singing the ancient unchanged words to popular songs of the time, such as 'Amaryllis,' 'Three colours in one,' 'The cowherds on the mountain.' This justifies us in conceiving that some fragments of wild chants may have been brought into modern shape and ordinance by those who allured the faithful to praise and prayer by recourse to mundane devices; such admission being easier to entertain than the idea that 'Az yashir Moshe' (The song of Moses) is the veritable intact hymn of 'the Red Sea,' as sung by the ancient Hebrews.

What curious, capricious gleams of twilight are let in, so often as we pry into the mysteries of old time! The Christians, no doubt, were largely indebted for their melodies to the Hebrews; and they were willing, says Clement of Alexandria,[9] to give the harp and lyre a part in their social festivities, 'because David played on them,' but prohibited the flute, because that instrument 'had been used in the service of idolatry.' Yet Christians did not refuse to avail themselves of the services of the organ—an instrument no less pagan, which, resolved into its primitive elements, is merely a box of flutes—an improved application of the pipes of Pan.

[9] Cited by M. de Sola.

Certain, again, it is that the Church, which pressed into its service so many of the forms of Ancient Mythology (and some of these not of the purest), which allowed superstitions connected with Venus to glide into the worship of the Madonna, made far ampler and more open use of the Greek modes—Lydian, Doric, and Phrygian—by adopting them as chants, than of these Hebrew melodies, so far as can be traced. The only example which I can call to mind is No. 35 in M. de Sola's Collection, 'Yar Shemang,' in which may be traced the germ of the Latin Christmas hymn, 'Adeste fideles,' known familiarly as the 'Portuguese hymn.'

The use of ancient Hebrew music made by modern composers may be described as small and unimportant, its capabilities and temptations considered. It is less known, indeed, than what may be called the civilised ritual music belonging to any other religion, and, unlike that of the Roman Catholic, Lutheran, and even Greek churches, has never passed into our concert-rooms. It is true that 'an entertainment,' with a view of presenting the treasures of the Synagogue to Christian consideration, was attempted here some years since by Mr. Henry

Phillips, but it was too empirically prepared and imperfectly carried out, to do any justice to a subject so wide and peculiar, or to engage the attention of a public so averse to novelty as the public of England. The silence, at first view, seems stranger to those who bear in mind how valuable have been the contributions both to creative and executive art which we owe to the children of Israel. Without hyperbole, they may be said to have inherited the garment of praise and the spirit of melody; but it is, perhaps, a necessary consequence of their position in the world, that while they have been the bondsmen of others, they have timidly, or from jealousy, hidden away their own treasures, and clinging close to their faith in private, have been compelled to lend themselves to the works of the Philistines before the world. Splendidly as Braham delivered the final recitatives in Handel's 'Israel,' his greater triumphs were in 'The Messiah' and 'Luther's Hymn.' I cannot call to mind that Pasta, the greatest singer of Hebrew origin who ever drew breath, in any moment of her career, sacred or profane, asserted the individuality of the faith of her ancestors, superbly as she delivered the music of the Romish Church. So, again, possibly the most powerful and sudden burst of Rachel's dramatic fire was when she rushed on the stage in Corneille's ' Polyeucte,' with the enthusiastic ' *Je crois!* ' which proclaimed her ready for the rack and flames of Christian martyrdom.

It is true that certain modern German critics and historians, with an ingenious subtlety in torturing speculation, have permitted themselves to use such a phrase as ' tic Hebraique,' applied to the works of musicians of Hebrew origin : and this they assume as a national characteristic, to be discerned in the music of two men, in their art as opposite as the poles—Mendelssohn and Meyerbeer. The vivacity of the former, as evidenced by the rapidity of certain of his movements, and his frequent and happy employment of *staccato* phrases, is ascribed to a feverish, uneasy restlessness, ever in search for illicit effect. The only analogous manifestation I can recall in the works of Meyerbeer lies in the theme of his overture to ' Marguerite d'Anjou,' which I have heard contemptuously styled ' Jews' music.' A more ridiculous piece of prophecy after the fact, of forcing a definition to fit circumstances, could hardly be cited. Of all the animated artists who ever lived, Mendelssohn, when need was, was the most placid, the most

serene, the one who sacrificed the least of his own
independence to effect, as all his sacred, and much of
his secular, music remains to attest. That he had
tastes in harmony tending towards mannerism, is
not to be denied ; but the sole trace of Hebrew influence that I can think of, in all the body of music
he poured out, is in a few portions of his ' Athalie '
music. These as well befitted a Jewish story as did
the faëry tone his ' Midsummer Night's Dream,'—
as did the wild billowy heavings of the North Sea
his ' Hebriden ' overture—as did the ' Saltarella '
finale to his symphony which we call Italian—as did
the perfect yet pensive beauty, thrown into no
modern forms, which pervades portions of his choral
music to ' Antigone and Œdipus.'

The disparaging criticism has a shade more of
pertinence if it be applied to the music of Meyerbeer ;
that most feverish of all seekers, that most obsequious
of men resolute on conciliating favour at any price,
who absolutely, by this time-serving want of self-
dependence, so frittered away and distracted the
musical genius born within him, that many have
denied its existence. The entire contrast between
him and the master with whom illiberal sarcasm has
tied him up, could not be better proved than by the

first four bars of his 'Pater Noster,' in the last of which the repose, yet awe, which the words convey is entirely disturbed by the sudden transition or leap in the melody—effective, it may be, but hardly devotional. But let the great qualities and defects imputed to his peculiar people have been ever so strong in the man, I am as unable to find any echoes from the synagogue in his music, as in the music of his great fellow-student under the fantastic and empirical Abbé Vogler, of whom I shall have to speak more than once—Carl Maria von Weber.

From the Hebrews, an opulent and refined and musical people,—a people, withal, without a country—it is an abrupt, yet not wholly unnatural transition, to pass to another world of homeless wanderers, in diametrically opposite circumstances—the world of Gipsies. By this passage we are transported from luxury, wealth, an elaborate cultivation, into what may be called the howling wilderness of Art : a wilderness, however, teeming with interesting natural productions. I cannot do better than avail myself of the distinction traced by the Abbé Liszt, in his book on the Music of the Bohemians, which, wild and exaggerated though it be in style, contains much ingenious specu-

lation and more curious anecdote. He points out
that whereas, throughout all the circumstances of
their dispersion, and persecution consequent on their
isolation from the families of Christendom, the
Hebrews have retained their individuality by living
under the strictest subjection to antique rule and
law; the Gipsies have vindicated their peculiar
character by irreclaimable lawlessness; and, while
wandering about as chartered or unchartered liber-
tines among civilised folk, have clung obstinately to
certain characteristic habits, which are merely
expressions of lawless disobedience. Whereas the
ancient people possesses a grand language and a
Book which, apart from its origin, outbuys all the
books of the world, the ancient swarm has only a
jargon, and what may be without offence called *a
slang* literature, of which little if any written record
exists. And this separation of two noticeable
families of the human race—a separation as wide as
that of day from darkness, howbeit, in one respect
the two families are similarly situated—is in no
point more signally illustrated than in their dealings
with the art here treated. Whereas the Hebrews
have inherited or got together a body of religious
music distinct in its form, and excellent in its glory;

whereas, during a century past, they have contri-
buted to modern art some of the most complete
creators and interpreters that have ever existed—
such as Mendelssohn, Meyerbeer, Pasta, Rachel,
Braham, Ernst, Joachim, Moscheles;—the members
of the gipsy horde, though they universally show
aptitude and proficiency to a certain point, in the
devices that charm ear and eye, never seem able to
advance beyond indication and capricious wilfulness.
Gipsy music is of very limited value, if disconnected
from the gipsy performance of it, and from the
impression made by it on those who, for the sake of
sensation, will endure and relish anything, no matter
how eccentric it be. Comparatively few gipsy tunes,
save a Russian or Hungarian dance or two, which
possibly own some such parentage, have passed into
the world's store of melodies. I think Schubert is
the only great composer, and after him the Abbé
Liszt, in his 'Rhapsodies Hongroises,' who has
used them heartily; and close as is the resemblance of tribe with tribe—whether the folk are
to be found burrowing in the cliffs embossed with
wine and oleander and Indian fig, that face the
Alhambra at Granada, or threading their tedious
way across some Transylvanian waste—it is not

easy to define or specify in what the style of their music consists, beyond a vocal lawlessness which marks its Oriental origin, and a certain wild fertility of improvisation in which the instrumental players are encouraged to give vent to their fancies as they rise.

The voices of the gipsy singers are generally detestable; and this may not be altogether owing to the coarse, feverish, comfortless lives they lead, or their fondness for drink :—the natural poverty and offence may belong to the race. I can call to mind nothing so intolerable as the hoarse yet piercing screams emitted by a troupe whose performances I heard in Granada. How, with so much obvious feeling for rhythm as the people possess, they can endure discords so atrocious, is a matter only to be explained by the separation which certainly exists in music between sense of tone and sense of time. I was assured that these were practitioners of the lowest class. They were, however, possibly none the less genuine for not being trained, tamed, and sophisticated for public exhibition, as are the more notorious gipsies of the Triana at Seville. And indeed, with reference to this very subject, the Abbé Liszt tells us that the real, pure (or rather impure)

E

gipsy style is to be heard in greater perfection among the hordes of Hungary than in Russia. The far-famed gipsies of Moscow—among the most deadly and dangerous sirens a corrupt society has ever encouraged—are, he tells us, made up for show. Of all showy things, show nationality is the worst.

The race has favourite instruments of its own. The violin, in some form more or less primitive, goes everywhere. To this the gipsies add the cymbal; not the pair of Mambrino's basins clashed, or quietly thrilled, one against the other, which we call by that name, but a sort of wicked dulcimer whipped by the player. The name clings to instruments of its class, handled by vagrant musicians, as does the name *vielle*, *viola*, or *gironda* among those of the hurdy-gurdy family. There was one, only a few years past, played on by a poor old woman in the London streets. Perhaps the name may be accepted as defining a harsh and stinging tone :—' *cembalo* ' defines a harpischord in Italian. The Hungarian gipsy cymbʟl, the Abbé Liszt says — on what authority I cannot ascertain—dates from the fifteenth century. The player on it shares, with the first violin the task of bringing out and lengthening cer-

tain passages, in accordance with the humour of
the moment. The Abbé gives curious anecdotes of
these wild and lawless people when domesticated in
Transylvanian households. It was their habit to
accompany armies on the march as musicians so late
as the beginning of the last century. But I fancy
(save in such a ministry to illicit luxury as they
offer in Russia) the palmy days of the gipsy
musicians are over, and that we shall hear no more
of such prodigal doings as those of the Hungarian
noble who bound up a vagrant violin-player's arm
in a bundle of bank-notes. Year by year they must
fade out, and be absorbed into the world of more
civilised races.

I cannot close these paragraphs without pointing
out, as among many marking characteristics of the
kind which distinguish him, the felicitous adoption
of the wild style of gipsy music by Weber, in his
'Preciosa' march. Nor has Signor Verdi, whose
use of local material is habitually slight and thrown
into the most conventional of forms, been without a
touch of the right spirit, thrown into the beginning
and close of the chorus which opens the second act
of 'Il Trovatore.' Those who recollect the audacious
incorrect performances of M. Reményi, the violinist,

who for a time sojourned in London and formed
part of Her Majesty's private band, may recall, as
the sole merit which they possessed, some traces of
the wild humour and fire with which the music
of this vagabond race may be credited.   Gipsy
music is a weed of the strangest form, colour, and
leafage; one hardly to be planted in any orderly
garden.

Lastly, with reference to Eastern origin and influences, the music of Spain must be touched on : a
subject full of perplexity to all those persons who
comfort themselves with a theory of the connection of
the arts. Such a theory is utterly untenable as regards
music, supposing connection to imply contemporaneous existence ; and its futility can be proved no-
where more completely than by reference to the
music of the Peninsula. What need is there to
revert to the days of Spain's pomp and power ?
What need to recall, that after Eastern domination
had ceased there (how wonderfully represented by
its monuments !) [10] there could arise and flourish in

[10] The meagreness, not to say absence, of what may be called
representative architecture in Spain, subsequent to the departure
of the Moors, is one among the many anomalies with which the
student of art has to deal. It is true that the Gothic style in
church-building was modified to some degree by the introduction

the land a school of painters, of dramatists, of poets,
of novelists, who by their individuality challenged—
if they did not surpass—their brethren in every
kingdom of Europe; and these, not always artists
starved because society had no room for them—but
men cherished by munificent persons who de-
lighted to surround themselves with everything that
is refined, pleasure-giving, and luxurious. Yet more:
the Roman Catholic Church, to whose patronage,
as distinct from prescience, music owes so much,
had always one of her most august thrones in Spain.
and round about that throne, her cathedrals with
their reliquaries—her holy houses with inmates ready
to lay every gift they possessed on the altar. Further,
that the people of Spain inherit a graceful aptitude
for receiving art, might to this day be predicated
from their noble bearing, from their picturesque
fancies of colour in dress, from their inborn, inbred
courtesy of demeanour, such as the traveller finds
among few, if any, continental folk.

of the *Plateresco* humour; but that applies to fashion in decoration,
not to form of structure; and the wonderful piled-up shrines and
altars to be seen in the great and gorgeous Spanish cathedrals
hardly outdo similar specimens which might have been cited so far
north as the Lower Rhineland, say from the churches of Xanten
and Neuss. The question, I repeat, is full of perplexing inconsistency.

Nevertheless, Spain, with its Alhambra, and its wondrous church (once mosque) at Cordova, its Alcazar of Seville, its later cathedrals, its splendid school of painters—headed by Velasquez—and its affluent and gorgeous world of drama (one which has only of late been fully displayed to us), has not yielded a single universal name to the annals of written music, whether the same be ecclesiastical or theatrical, save the one of Morales; and his to all intents and purposes is a name, and nothing more. That during the past half-century Spain has given to Europe a family of representative artists—the Garcia family—whose power, genius, and originality have printed a permanent trace in the record of methods of vocal execution and ornament, may be in some sort the exception which proves the rule.

And yet so early as the fifteenth century, Spain possessed an accomplished theoretical historian in Ramis or Rames de Pareja: a man of such mark and repute, that he was sent for from Salamanca to Italy, by Pope Nicholas the Fifth, to take the direction of a music-school at Bologna *la dotta,* in which learned town he died. A century later, Salinas, the blind musician, probably the greatest among blind musicians on record, was invited by the Cardinal Archbishop of Compostella to Rome, and there cultivated, honoured, and made an *Abate* of Saint Pancrazius, of Rocca Scalegna, by His Holiness Paul the Fourth. The work by Salinas, written in Latin and published in 1577, appears to be in advance of its time, especially in its treatment and recognition of our subject— national melody.   Some of the Spanish and Moorish specimens cited therefrom by Mr. Graham,[11] noted (of course, from ear) by Salinas, are curious, as not indicating any of those peculiarities of interval and rhythm which we have come to consider as character- istic of Spanish music.   Here is a tune on six notes of the octave, as formal as if Moore had fitted it to his song.

LET ERIN REMEMBER THE DAYS OF OLD.

This, in its simplicity and absolute orderliness of interval, is akin to the phrases of Turkish melody given in a former page of this essay.

Now, seeing that the Peninsula is by nature so

[11] Art. ‘Music,’ *Encyclopædia Britannica*, ed. 7.

richly endowed, and is manned by a population so courteous, so different in matters of truth and untruth from other southern folk; and seeing that music has been there so largely called on to take part in its festivals, whether they be priestly or lay, public or private, and that dramatic art has been there exhibited in a fertility and fluency unexampled and unparagoned in any country of Europe—one may well speculate why such a land should have never yielded a single European composer. And this fact is all the more singular, I repeat, since we know their drama not only to be full of varied character, but lyrical also, beyond the drama of any other country. The luxury of its high sentiments and intricate incidents, expressed in verbal rhythms of admirable euphony, without that tiresome sonority which must cloy, cannot be exceeded. My brother, Mr. J. R. Chorley, whose researches into the subject may be relied on,[12]—since, I am proud to say, they have been accepted and turned to account by the most ingenious and erudite scholars of the country—assured me that an occasional stage-song was probably supported by a guitar; that

[12] *Vide* his *Catalogo de Comedias y Autos de Frey Lope Felix de Vega Carpio*, written in Castilian and printed in Spain.

angels, supernatural personages, kings on their en-
trance, were solemnly announced by the sounds of a
sort of clarion; but that he has found no trace of
anything racy, original, or distinctive—reserving
such music as derives its origin from the dance.

This fact becomes doubly curious if the wild
music (so to say) of the country is considered.
Some of the old vocal melodies of the Peninsula bear
distinct traces of their lawless oriental origin: as,
for instance, the following, in which the symphonic
burthen is perfectly easy to detach from the words:

This specimen, which I have no reason to conceive impurely noted, contains a clear indication of that syncopation or suspense or pause which characterises Spanish national music: which may be said in some degree to enforce a spasmodic manner on the artist who is to deliver it. This effect I take to have been the '*Hocket*,' which term so puzzled Sir John Hawkins when he encountered it in one of the Cotton manuscripts, that he devoted half a page to dull guesses as to its meaning,[13] whereas the least

[13] There has been of late years a fashion to decry Burney as flippant and courtly—a flimsy musical historian—as compared with Hawkins. I can but say, that whereas the judgments and the facts of the former writer hold good, I have rarely consulted the latter with reference to any matter beyond the pale of his limited sympathies, without finding proofs of inexactness, attested by dogmatism, bearing out Johnson's definition of Sir John as a man habitually inexact. Witness his obtuse ignorance of the astounding identity betwixt the fugues of Kerl, printed among his specimens, with the

quickness or knowledge of French might have
assured him that the word was merely a mis-spelling
of '*Hocquet*' or '*Hiccup*,' which in homely phrase
represents musical syncopation.

A collection of hybrid tunes before me, gathered
in Cuba—a little book of the songs to this day sung
by the children going round, who make so joyous
and pretty a feature in the summer evening life at
Madrid—illustrate the definitions I have ventured to
lay down. They are either lawless, to the very verge
of barbarity, or vapid, stale, and inexpressive. Such

chorus ' Egypt was glad,' in Handel's ' Israel : '—Sir John professing
himself to be a weighty Handelian. Witness his assertion that
Dryden had destined his superb 'Alexander's Feast' to be set by
Henry Purcell; whereas the ode was not written till Purcell had
been dead two years! There will always be a public with whom
surliness passes for earnestness,—ponderosity of manner for depth
of thought—and dogmatic assertion for research. Save as regards
English cathedral music, I conceive Sir John Hawkins' History one
in no respect to be relied on. There is another signal instance of
his incorrectness in this very matter of Spanish music, in his
notation of the familiar *Fandango* (to which I shall return) used
by Gluck in his ballet, ' Dom Juan,' and by Mozart in his ' Nozze,'
as under.

By the above preposterous transcription everything like stateliness
of character is tamed out of the measure.

are the *Seguidillas* and *Modinhas* which in my young
days the rising gentlewomen of England, whose
Spanish was

Of the school of Stratford-atte-Bowe,

used to drawl out on an ill-conducted guitar; be-
lieving the same national, patriotic, and picturesque.

In continuation, attention may be called to some
modern specimens of composition in the national
style, where the antique semi-barbarous Spanish
wildness is turned to account by a distinguished
child of the soil— one thoroughly versed in the
science of 'high composition' (as the French
phrase it), Madame Viardot. But in her Spanish
melodies, the intervals and phrases will be found more
arresting by their strangeness, than charming by
any beauty. They speak of the vocal usages of a
land, with which those not pervaded by Oriental
predilections can only be brought to sympathise,
inasmuch as the palate may come to accept and enjoy
peculiar meats by the persuasion of habit and the
force of residence.

Capital, quaint, and altogether peculiar, is the
rhythmical, or dance music of Spain; its characteristics owing, if not their origin, their suggestion
to the national instrument, by aid of which the

queer, harsh cries of the singing voice are somehow
rudely methodised and brought into some order. One
must go to the Peninsula to know the uses and
privileges of the guitar. The pungency and adroitness of the performers on it are hard to overpraise,
and no less hard to define—including as they do,
tricks, preludings, modulations crude enough to make
a master of harmony's hair stand on end—instinct
the while with an irresistible spirit and vivacity to be
paralleled, it may be, but not to be exceeded under
any other sun. Some few of those who read these
paragraphs may recollect the guitar vagaries of
Senhor Huerta, who many years ago came into
England. But his guitar (so to say) had been tamed,
washed, and combed, as compared with the 'un-
feigned' guitar to be heard in Spanish cities, even in
these later days, and no doubt existing in nooks
and corners far more obscure, for the delectation and
the incitement of people of the soil. I shall never
forget an old blind creature whom I followed about
for several evenings in Madrid : a man who would
plant himself on the causeway, sitting with his feet
in the kennel, scrupulously clean in his linen,
totally engrossed with his guitar ; and who hardly
seemed to care if coppers were flung to him or not ;

and to whom the casual ready-to-hand audience of
common folk gathered round him (some arranging
themselves comfortably on the causeway and kennel
side, to listen, as folk do on a quay at Venice
or Chiozza to follow the tale of a story-teller),
sufficed for the contentment of the modest wants of
his vanity. In his preluding or fancy-work, a sort
of wild gloss and comment on some simple group of
notes, there rarely failed to be odd, unexpected
touches of harmonic modulation; but when he struck
off into a more regular melody, such as the one here
noted—

Spirited.

or when he engaged in a dance tune, not only was
his feeling for accent in itself excellent and provocative (and a feeling for accent is a thing which
great artists have laboured to acquire, and have died
without acquiring), but it seemed incited, and fed,
and sharpened, by the pungent sound of the strings,
and the thrum of the hand on the sounding-board,

till at last the excitement produced by that weak
old mendicant from his miserable chattel of an
instrument, amounted to an experience as peculiar as
it is pleasant to recall.

As another element in Spanish dance music, the
castanet is not to be overlooked, as working in magic
combination with those queer, poignant guitar
sounds; enabling the dancer to be in part his own
orchestra, and to excite himself, as did the faun of
antique mythology, by the sound of the pipes into
which he breathed as he leaped among the vines.
But the castanet is obviously a condiment to the
dance, more complete and comfortable than the
faun's reeds, seeing that motion must shorten the
breath. To the guitar and castanet is, in some
districts of Spain, added a clarinet of a coarse sort
—not, of course, undertaken by the dancer.

The entire exhibition bears a generically different
character from those of music and dancing belonging
to any other country.[14] In the Spanish measures
there is a certain dignity, never wholly thrown by,

[14] And yet there are coincidences not to be overlooked. The
dances of the north in 'tempo alla Polacca,' of which notice will
appear in a later page, with the freaks and whimsies not so much
allowed to as expected from the leader of the band, have a certain
affinity in their licence to the achievements of the Madrid guitar
player, and in their humour to that which he called up.

be the movement ever so brisk. Coarse, no doubt,
they become, when adopted by performers of an
inferior class—as all dances in which any Oriental
prompting lingers are apt to do—but in themselves,
the *Saraband* (the ' Moorish' Saraband, a feature not
formerly to be dispensed with at any English fair)
the *Fandango*, the *Bolero*, and a score of modified
varieties of these dances, the existence of which it is
sufficient to indicate, have a ' state' as well as an
' ancientry,' the like of which is to be found only in
the *Minuet* and the *Polonoise*: which two, be it noted,
have never been popular so much as courtly measures.
What can be more stately and pompous than the
well-known theme, transmogrified as we have seen
by Sir John Hawkins; employed first by Gluck in
his ballet of ' Dom Juan,' and subsequently by
Mozart in ' Le Nozze'?

There would seem to be something more than
usually attractive in this chain of notes : since it
recurred to Mendelssohn, as the theme of the *Finale*
to his second *Pianoforte Trio*, and more recently
still to M. Felicien David, in his ' Lalla Rookh'—

who has therefore been bitterly assailed as a pla-
giarist from Mendelssohn.

In another respect, the Spanish dances are peculiar: proving themselves akin to the spasmodic vocal
music characterised awhile since, and gaining character from pauses, syncopations, interruptions of
rhythm; such as the great school of South German
waltz composers—Lanner, Strauss, Labitzky, and
others—have turned to such admirable account.

To close this section of the inquiry in hand, a
definition may be ventured—to wit, that in the
National Music of Spain, whether vocal or instrumental, Eastern forms and influences are to be traced;
and that singularly little progress has been made in
the employment of these by the free musicians of the
Peninsula, as distinguished from the 'strict' ones
who have wrought daily and ineffectively under
ecclesiastical thraldom.   Betwixt Oriental traditions
and Papistical necessities, music in Spain has fallen

F

into a state of atrophy and apathy: these, however, be it remarked, amounting to no such recoil after a period of glorious production, such as is to be lamented by those who follow the story of Italian music.

MUSIC FROM THE SOUTH.

WHILE dealing with the subject of National Music, it seems to me that the diversities of handling which, with every change of the points of the compass, it requires, have hardly been sufficiently taken into account by the generality of those who have considered it. On passing from the east to the south, and thence to France, the amount of noticeable material which presents itself defies any attainable completeness in statement or classification. It is only possible to select a few leading characteristics, and those which have been the least dwelt on by previous historians and students.

Every child, from his cradle-days upwards, has heard of Italy as the land of music. The world is indebted to it for all that makes the beauty of the art, and for much of its science. The last reservation is made in recognition of the claims which have been put forward for Low-country musicians of science; claims not to be dismissed superficially, and thus not to be examined here. But, however the same

F 2

may be rated, the restrictions and inconsistencies to be noted in the being and in the doings of Italian art are as numerous as they are singular.

Overflowing with natural beauty, rich in historical associations, and in relics which set these forth; peopled by those who are brimful of natural aptitude and that quick nervous sensibility which is so important an element of genius,—Italy, compared with the North, has very little national music that does not come within the circle of regular art. Let us inquire, for a moment, whether some explanation of the fact is not to be found.

The authorities of the country early possessed themselves of all the relics of Paganism; these to be converted to the ecclesiastical purpose of subduing the spirits of men. When that most remarkable building, the cathedral of Torcello—now desolate and lonely, by the side of its accessory church, that of Santa Fosca—was built in the weed-grown island far among the Venetian lagoons, transparent slabs of alabaster were brought from afar to fill the windows, without obscuring daylight—glass then having no existence—and with them beautifully carved borders and patterns of Greek marble broken up to encrust the pulpit. The art of mosaic, too,

had already made some rude progress; though
orthodoxy had not so far settled the uses of the new
decoration, as to proscribe the intrusion of Charon
and his boat, transferred from the ancient mythology,
into the Christian artist's vision of 'the Last
Judgment.' There were—if there be not still—
stranger ensigns of a more sensual Pagan legend
than this to be seen in the churches of Southern
Italy. Thus, too, the barbaric chants—(that it would
be strange to find occurring among the Greeks, had
we not cause to deny the contemporaneous perfection
of the arts)—the 'modes of the lyre' which had
figured in the hymns to Jupiter or to Venus—which
had helped, as the people of Athens and Corinth
thought, to set off the odes of Pindar and the
choruses of the great dramatists—were appropriated,
arranged, and methodised, so as to serve in the form
of music's offerings to the rites of the Christian
temples, earliest established in Italy. It may be
that the land, harassed and heterogeneously peopled,
had nothing indigenous to offer.

Meanwhile, in Italy, from a remote period, there
may be traced, whether among churchmen or nobles,
indications of a gracious, liberal, and sympathising
spirit as regards art, to which love and honour are

due. And this did not take the form of patronage
so much as of participation ; so that music acquired
there a life, an aspect, and a position somewhat
different to those fought for or won by it during its
childish years in other countries. Very limited, it
may be suspected, was the amount of suggestion
furnished by the untutored people of Italy to their
churchmen and nobles. They, I repeat—as men n
authority, of a genial and artistic temperament,
which is for ever in search for culture and enrichment, should do—laid hold of the 'modes' of Greece,
improved on the instruments of the East, and accepted
aid from the Low Countries, and even, it has been said,
from England, for the perfecting of counterpoint :
just as they had laid hold of the marbles of Greece
and appropriated its mythologies in Christianised
forms.

Yet, with all this aid and protection, such music
as Italy possessed, during a long series of years,
may be asserted to have been as grim and ungracious
to the ear, as are the pictures of Cimabue and
Margharitone to the eye : valuable though both are
to the archæologist, drearily barbarous to such
moderns as have not been trained into the habits
of retrospective comparison belonging to antiquarian

pursuits. It may be remarked (as bearing on the
connection of the fine arts), that architecture in
Italy had got past the plight of the savage's
wigwam, or the natural grotto in which the people
of a persecuted sect might assemble covertly for
worship—had raised august buildings, which the
taste of our time appreciates and its workers
imitate—long ere the painter was, in his world,
superior to the wigwam artists: longer still, ere the
musician had ceased in his gloomy psalmody to
correspond with the rude and awful catacomb.
Further, whereas architect and painter, once having
found their use and level, established principles and
canons of art, and thenceforward each, in his own
great period, walked steadily forward from skill to
skill, from beauty to beauty; it is noticeable that in
music the progress of inborn genius, as regulated
and quickened by acquired science, was slack and
timid in its adjustment.

But it may be divined by something more than
random guess-work. The history of our art would
reveal the fact that the nobles of Italy, whether
ecclesiastic or lay, did far more to leaven the people
with musical traditions—to quicken them with
musical impulses—than the people themselves could

do, while paying tribute to the nobles, to suggest
the riches of the soil on and out of which the
palaces of the country, whether priestly or lay, were
built and flourished.

Such a speculation leads into another one—the
limits and value of the union of patronage with
participation, including practical amateurship, in
art.   Great, no doubt, was the impetus given to
music by such rulers as the Medici at Florence ; by
such a prince as the Prince of Venosa, who wrote
madrigals in advance of his time ; by such a pontiff
as Palestrina's master, the Pope Marcellus (Pius the
Fourth) ; by such a cardinal as Monsignore Ottoboni,
to whom Corelli, long his household friend, be-
queathed his treasures ; by such a patrician as
Marcello of Venice, whose setting of the first fifty
Psalms of David is a work of permanent value ; by
such a group of *dilettanti,* belonging to our own
days, as the Belgiojoso family, so influential in
Lombardy.   And yet it may be predicated that this
patronage and participation of cultivated and noble
persons, who naturally preferred to deal with such
works of art as were complete, and in some
accordance with the fashions of the hour, tended
towards the transformation, if not the effacement

of such natural material as may have existed among
the subject folk of Italy.

Because, to continue, there is danger, with this
patronage of art, of insincerity, if not decay, entering
into the artist's thoughts, and consequent seeming
and conventionality into the works which are their
product. I think this may be perceived throughout
the whole story of Italian art. Michael Angelo's
plan of St. Peter's, after having been altered again
and again by thwarting influences, could be conclu-
sively spoiled in what should have been its main
feature, by the mean and heavy frontispiece of
Carlo Maderno : his sculptures, the only ones in
which the Titans of antique sculpture were matched
by a Titan as strong in his own modern world as
they were in their mythologies, could be displaced
in favour by the fluttering, meretricious sentimental-
ities of Bernini. And so, from this illustration to
come into our own peculiar world, in the dealings of
Italian patronage with music, I have detected no
settled recognition of a dawn as of an awakening ;
nor of a morn as a beginning ; nor of a noon as of
a fulfilment ; nor of an afternoon as an enrichment ;
nor of the more tranquil glories of evening leading
on to the solemn splendours of night : no fixed

principle of that reverence for the past which
makes the inevitable work of Time's progress pro-
gressive, not destructive, so much as one of obsequious
and licentious conformity to the impulses of the
moment.   Surely, there is no need that change in
creative efforts should imply disdain or forgetfulness
of what has been.   But, partly from the driftings of
fashion, partly from political circumstance, partly
from an unreasoning impatience of temperament,
the art of music in Italy has fallen into a singular
state of dilapidation.   There is hardly one solitary
masterpiece of ancient date—I except not the perfect
works of Palestrina, in their style unapproached—
which is cherished or known beyond the musty
circle of antiquaries.   This, it is to be considered,
may be no unimportant cause, why in Italy all
music has virtually merged in the theatre, as the
place where the tempers and emotions of the hour
are provided for and mirrored.   Instrumental composition may be said to have only a nominal existence
in one or two towns.   The Church, after having by
her mysteries and miracle-plays set opera a-going,
found her a far too potent Dalilah not to be pressed
into her service, and turned to good account, as
maintaining a close hold on the weak and the

sensual. Whether the scene be St. Mark's at
Venice, or Michael Angelo's noble church built
above the baths of Diocletian at Rome, or the
gorgeous and complete cathedral of Monreale above
Palermo, or the strange temple in the little town,
which loads the island in the lovely lake of Orta;
one and the same tale is to be heard everywhere:
organ-playing, with the ambling *four-in-a-bar* bass
which so affronted Mendelssohn, ridiculous enough
to make Frescobaldi turn in his grave—vocal
melodies repugnantly frivolous enough to call up
the solemn Pope Marcellus, once more to drive the
doves and the money-changers from the house of
worship.

And it may be observed that the vitiation of one
branch of any given art, connived at on the poor
excuse of creating a momentary sensation, is surely
attended by retributive decay in every other one. It is
a striking warning, in a land which may be to-day
as rich in genius as it ever was, to consider to what
a pass the headlong pursuit of sensation, no matter
how false, so it be only sufficiently exciting, has
brought Italian music's last stronghold, the theatre.
Ignorance and Rant now reign, where Skill and
Beauty were formerly King and Queen. It is not

possible to conceive false exaggeration carried further by fickleness. Cimarosa is hardly known by
name. Paisiello is totally defunct as a celebrity:
his charming 'Nina Pazza,' in which Pasta
was as charmingly pathetic as she was awful
in 'Medea,' having been reset by the inefficient
Signor Coppola, whose setting is already deservedly
forgotten; Signor Rossini tolerated as *rococo*, or else
miserably misrepresented by a crew of the incom-
petent bawlers, who have replaced the splendid
vocalists of past times; Bellini the graceful, and
Donizetti the fertile (and more than fertile, as his
operas 'La Fille du Régiment,' 'Don Pasquale,'
and the final act of 'La Favorite,' show) shelved; because fashion, or dilettantism, or Italian sympathy,
or call it whatever the world pleases, has run riot
to bray from trumpets or to thump on drums, that
Signor Verdi is the one prophet of Italian opera.
And since this paragraph was penned, the waning
of the coarse light of his star is pretty distinctly to
be observed. It is hardly possible to imagine his
violence outdone by any successor; yet this would
seem to be the law of Italian movement in such
shows of art as are to be popular.

I have now to advert to a potent influence of

diametrically opposite quality to the one descanted
on; an influence which figures as a permanent
feature in Italian taste and manners, unchanged by
any passing rage for a Michael Angelo, or a Bernini—for a Cimarosa, a Paisiello, a Rossini, a Bellini,
a Verdi. This is the curious indifference which the
people of that lovely land display for the beauty of
nature;—and again, their poverty in such descriptive faculty, and quaint fantasy, as impart so much
racy variety to the forms taken by Northern national
art. This can hardly be a case of climate, so much
as the weakness, if not altogether the want of an
especial sense. The absence or presence of this
has, I hold, much to do with the character of national
melody, as generating national music. How strange
does this seem to us Northerns, who, allowing their
utmost inspiration to mist and snow, have nothing
in scenery to emulate the splendour and variety of
the South. Think of Titian's birth-land, the 'Pays
de Cadore;' some of whose features, it is true, he
reproduced in certain of his pictures—as for instance the St. Peter Martyr. Think of the northern
lakes, the upper part of the Lago d' Iseo, round and
above Lovere, to be expressly commemorated;—think
of the entire line of Italian coast, so fascinating in

its mixture of cliff, headland, and ocean;—think of
those towns of central Italy, not a few of which are
hung on shaggy and steep hill-sides, as Forsyth the
traveller said of Cortona, 'like a picture against a
wall;'—think of such a district as Calabria, so bold
and fierce in its volcanic rifts and crevices, yet teeming as though Bacchus and Ceres had disputed from
above every inch of ground on which Pluto from
below could plant his foot. And then think, with
every rich and picturesque object which could delight
a painter's eye, or garnish a poet's rhyme, how few
and far between are the allusions in the literature of
Italy to the characteristic glories of a land by
nature so gorgeously endowed.

This scantiness of imagination may be said in
some measure to pervade the popular literature of
Italy. As compared with that of the Northern people,
it is poor in shadows, in omens, in goblins. The
folk, it is true, have an implicit belief in the evil eye,
and in the *ombra della casa* of the South—otherwise
the 'Bella 'Mbriana,' Neapolitan corruption of
Ombriana—who is supposed (to quote a letter from an
English resident in Italy, addressed to the *Athenæum*)
'to be the tenant of every house in many a village
in the bay, and to exercise a considerable influence

over the destinies of a family.' She is a distant
kinswoman of the Scotch Brownie and the Irish
Cluricaune—devoted, touchy, or troublesome, in pro-
portion as she is treated civilly or the reverse. She
is propitiated accordingly, and the peasants (says the
authority above referred to) make a point of bidding
her good night, with, it may be, as much fear as
love. Nor must one forget the fairy Morgana, to
whose enchantments have been ascribed those
magical atmospheric effects, which make Sicily and
its skies and sea so charming; neither the Orco of
Venice, so picturesquely presented by Madame
Dudevant in one of her best Venetian romances. But
the list of the Italian beings of superstition at best
makes but a poor show. As for witches, those under
the walnut tree at Benevento, whose gambols
inspired Paganini the wizard with one of his
quaintest *fantasias*, are almost the only ones whose
reputation has crossed the Alps. The supernatural
terrors of 'Udolpho' were conjured up by no native
romancer, but by a gentle, retired Englishwoman,
amid the fogs of the bad climate which the Southerns
hold in such effeminate disdain.

An exception to the above limitation might be
thought to present itself in the 'Fiabe' or super-

naturally grotesque plays of Carlo Gozzi, which for so long a period kept so strong a hold on the play-goers of Venice; and to which may be ascribed those *extravaganzas*, the popularity of which has not yet altogether died out in the minor theatres of Vienna, and to cater for which Shikaneder the buffoon tempted Mozart to write his 'Zauberflöte.' For in them will be found that power over the marvellous which becomes strange when united with command over the deepest, most serious passions which thrill the heart and frame of humanity. But neither 'Il Corvo,' the scene of which is the imaginary city of Frattombrosa; nor 'L'Amore delle Tre Melarancie;' nor 'Turandot,' a Chinese legend, for which, on its being arranged for the German stage by Schiller, Weber wrote his characteristic overture; nor 'Il Re Cervo,' the king of Serendib; nor 'La Donna Serpente,' the scene of whose gambols was Tiflis; nor 'Zobeide,' a story of the city of Samandal; nor 'Il Mostro Turchino,' another Chinese fable; nor 'I Pitocchi Fortunati,' a tale of Samarcand; nor 'L'Augellino Belverde,' belonging to the unknown capital of Monterotondo; nor 'Zeim,' the ruler of the spirits whose home was Balsora—represent native forms, usages, and beliefs, more than do the majority of the fairy tales collected by Straparola. They belong to outlying worlds of fancy, in which nationality has small part.

To look at another side of the subject, it may be observed that whenever Southern influences have leavened the literature and art of any given country, the same communicated torpor in regard to picturesque, as distinguished from classical and academical imagery, is to be remarked. Wordsworth, intense in his love for nature, and consummate in his knowledge of the subject, pointed out how, during a long period, our world of poetry suffered from the domination of foreign fashions, imported from among a people who, while loud in complaint of the harsh glooms of our northern climate, religiously bar out the summer sun, turning noon into sleepy night, and shrink from exertion or fatigue in search of natural beauty. But when Wordsworth indicated with a discriminating hand the time of awakening in English literature to the minute observation of nature, he would have been more correct had he described it as a time of revival; seeing that the faculty so sparingly diffused among the Italians is confessed in the works of all our great poets. If Chaucer, Shakspeare, Spenser, Milton, had as close an intimacy with the stately groves and temples of Greek and Roman art, as was ever enjoyed by those to whom they may be said to have been household words and home associations,—the first could write his freshest verse concerning the sweet season of Spring, with its fresh May blossoms ; the second had eyes to note the habits of

The temple-haunting martlet

as well as the moonlight sleeping on the bank at Portia's Belmont ; the third could paint the Den of Error ; the fourth, besides commemorating in a line of rare music, the

Autumnal leaves of Vallombrosa,

could produce the gallery of landscapes in 'L'Allegro,' the like of which exists not in all the picture galleries of Italian poetry. If these mighty men were aware of Parnassus and Tempe, they knew no less lovingly and well the secrets of moorland and meadow ; the wonders of the deep ; the visionary glories of the firmament. And the case is still more strongly made out, if, from the trained masters of poetry, we turn to the rude, popular ballad-mongers of this island. Let us look (as the first illustration which comes to hand) at the songs of Scotland ; and we shall find the braes of one locality, and the shaws of another, and the riggs of barley belonging to a third, commemorated in quaint phraseology, but with memory's genuine affection, by some native peasant songster. There is no song of Tivoli, none of the Lake of Como, so far as I have yet found. The gondoliers of Venice used to chant, but what?—strophes by Tasso. It is true, that among the words to their popular songs which so strangely resemble one another, favourite localities will be named—most frequently a church, as San Basso, Sandegola (Santo Giovanni Decollato); but these only sparingly, as compared with the harpings on 'Love, still love,' the one theme dwelt on by them with untiring unction and fervour. The *Stornelli* of Tuscany are open to the same remark; being, the while, more shrewd and proverbial, and less picturesque. The songs of the *Lazzaroni* and fishermen of Naples are fuller of whimsy and impudence, perhaps, but not of local colour. Of course, in the popular tunes of Naples, as well as of Venice, the sound of the boat, with its cadence of rowers, is ever and again to be heard. And the rhymesters make great use of the moon, for beneath the moon the lovers' serenades are given. But the varieties, I repeat, of what may be called pictorial themes, either in Italian words or music, are very few and restricted in their scope. It will be found that in opera the amount of descriptive music, as compared with that of sentiment and passion, is a mere nothing. Whereas Handel tried to represent in opera and oratorio, birds, fountains, the sun standing still, the darkness which might be felt, the Red Sea cleft by a miracle;—the composers of the South painted in sound with great timidity. There may be descriptive music in Cimarosa's operas, but they were rather devoted to stilted classical declamation, or the threadbare buffoonery of Harlequin's book. His galloping horse in the well-known air, ' Pria che spunti ' from ' Il Matrimonio ' is hardly in any known equestrian step. There is little descriptive music, strictly to speak, in Signor Rossini's Italian operas, save in ' La Donna del Lago,' in the last act of ' Otello,' and the ponderous introduction of ' Mosè,' where a thick darkness broods over the scene. That the greatest of modern composers had an acute and real appreciation of the peculiarities of national music, was proved in his French opera, ' Guillaume Tell,' in which the local colour and the use of the national melodies of the hill-country are perfect and unique. There is nothing in opera comparable to the second act of that opera; but it

was written for France, not for Italy, and written to
a stupid book, setting forth a great transaction.   In
Bellini's operas the dim introduction to the Druidical
tragedy of 'Norma' may be cited : in Donizetti's
little beyond the 'Barcarole' in 'Marino Faliero,' the
Savoyard's tune to his hurdy-gurdy in 'Linda,' the
Swiss song in 'Betly,' and the convent (or fourth)
act of 'La Favorita,' which having been impossible,
in Italy, under censorship, was written, as was
'Guillaume Tell,' for France.   In Signor Verdi's
works, I can but call to mind a barcarole in 'I due
Foscari,' another in 'Les Vêpres Siciliennes,' a
sunrise attempted in 'Attila,' and some use of the
genuine gipsy drawling closes in the anvil chorus of
his 'Il Trovatore.'   Nothing can be paler and more
puerile than the music given by him to the weird
sisters in his 'Macbeth.'

It is important that the above characteristics,
distinctions, and examples should be borne in mind,
while dealing with the form and bearing of national
music in Italy.   Let me now specify a few features
which are of special and marking interest.

From the Sicilies the land appears to have derived what may be called its pastoral music ; having a
peculiar rhythm and humour of its own, which have

been accepted and employed throughout Europe. The rhythm, it is true, is indicated as Moorish among the specimens cited by Salinas, the Spanish writer :

The dance which closes Monteverde's 'Orfeo,' one of the oldest operas of which we have any distinct cognizance—somewhat in the Siciliana style when played slow—is called *Moresca*. What, if this tune be some old relic of the East, which passed into Sicily as did the Pan's reeds of the Greeks ?

In any event, the instrument by aid of which the *Siciliana* style and form of national melody was imported into the world of trained music, was nothing more or less than the offspring of the primitive and mythological reeds of Pan, improved and assisted by mechanical discoveries. To dance and to blow a melody in one and the same operation, is a hard task ; and thus, the idea of filling Pan's pipes with winds from another agency than that of the breath, was carried out by the bag added to the reeds, and inflated by the elbow of the player: and thus I think the bagpipe, which some will object to hear called 'the shepherd's pipe,' took the form which it has since then worn as the shepherd's companion throughout a large portion of Europe.

I confess to a small kindness for the bagpipe, harsh, crude, and illicit as all its concords and discords are. The drone, otherwise ground bass, disconcerts the melody it supports; but, in its wild way, and in the open air, produces the effect of combination.

It is to sounds drawn from this bagpipe, sometimes in accompaniment to tuneless voices, by the bright-eyed, dark-skinned, dirty, shaggy, rural folk of Calabria, and of the Roman Campagna, that may be ascribed the perpetuation of that peculiar melody, the name of which has become a musical term. When the amiable and gracious Corelli wrote his 'Nativity concerto,' he reproduced, 'with a difference,' the tunes which these primitive herdsmen have been long used to play before the street-shrines of the Madonna at Christmas time. Handel, that most acute and royal of appropriators, whose plagiarisms and pilferings were as shameless as his genius was glorious, laid hands on one of the most popular of these *Pifferari* tunes, printed in old

English collections as a dance, to serve the turn of his 'Pastoral symphony' in the 'Messiah'; music in which (to quote from the Goethe and Zelter correspondence), 'one feels the star-light.' The same character of melody, with disregard of the drone bass, was exquisitely called out for the same situation by John Sebastian Bach in his Christmas oratorio. Beethoven, again, though he broke away from the traditional triple *tempo*, used the Sicilian shepherds' drone in his 'Pastoral symphony.' It has often occurred to me that the theme of Signor Rossini's delightful 'Di tanti palpiti' in 'Tancredi,' notoriously derived from a national tune, bears not indistinct traces of *Pifferari* origin; though the theme, of course, has been 'rhymed and twisted' so as to alter its character. Thus, it may be proved that from an instrument and a dancing measure, was planted in Italy one of the first types of rhythmical measure, as distinguished from harmonised chant; since, if the above speculations be tenable, the *Siciliana* bore an earlier date than the lauds or sacred canticles or than the madrigals accompanied by less savage instruments, which kept alive the Italian towns on festival days. The pastoral *alla Siciliana* may well be called the tune of Rome.

The memory of these lauds and canticles, sung on holidays by confraternities in procession—sometimes by nobles, sometimes by artisans—unlike that of the *Siciliana*, has thoroughly passed away. Yet, at the beginning of the last century, according to Crescembini, they figured bravely at the Roman jubilee; and the morning after Burney arrived in Florence, so late as 1770, he had the treat of hearing them singing a cheerful matin hymn in three parts, as they passed his lodgings in grand procession, 'dressed in a whitish uniform, with burning tapers in their hands.' How far this cheerful hymn was ancient or modern, there is no discovering. It is obvious, however, that—apart from music which was to be danced to—harmony predominated in the art long before melody took anything like that form and order of symmetrical beauty which so many absurd pedants, fancying themselves innovators, are at the time present trying to destroy, as something puerile and obsolete. The sacred lauds and secular madrigals were largely accompanied by instruments, and pretty much alike in character—bearing traces of the old influences and tones of Paganism : dry and shapeless, whether music was called in to enhance the solemnity of a rite of worship, or to grace

such revels as the beauties of the ' Decameron ' held,
when by aid of lute and pipe and *tiorba*, Fiordelisa
and Pampinea and their gay company beguiled the
time of pestilence.   Such life as existed was not to
be found in the *Carol*—to admit that word as a corruption of *corale* or church chant—so much as in
the *Ballad*, which again is derived from *ballata*—a
song with dance.   Among the first specimens in
which traces of form occur are the *fal-lal-la* burdens,
danced as well as sung.   In this specimen, the well-
known one by Gastoldi, which Burney printed
(observe, in triple time), something of the flow of
modern Italian melody is prophesied.

That was a great day for national Italian music,
when the church and the stage parted company;
when the people ceased to be contented with Biblical
histories and mysteries acted in places of public

worship; when the *improvisatori* and drolls who
rode in the Thespian cart, with their mother-wit and
mother poetry, struck out a new entertainment and
gave to the common folk a festival of their own, as
some equivalent for the costly spectacles which the
liberal and opulent bespoke for their palaces. Since
that time, however, the street-songs of Italy, with
some few exceptions, have always more or less
partaken of the theatrical style; have always been,
more or less, an exhibition of trained art. The instruments have remained comparatively uncouth and
simple, but the vocalists have been in the greatest
request who could reproduce the favourite stage-tune
of the hour and the favourite style of stage execution.
What may be called, then, characteristic or irregular
music, such as to this day flourishes pure and simple
in other districts, has in Italy faded into a monotonous and characterless tepidness—with some exceptions, I repeat, now to be specified.

The most remarkable of these, as to form, may be
referred to the Bay of Naples and the lagoons of
Venice, where the humour of the people has kept
alive something distinct and suggestive, owing
nothing to church or palace. The first of these to
be mentioned brings us once again to the dance,

within the spell of the *tarantella*, and the sound
of what may be called a gipsy instrument—that
small provocative drum with bells, the tambourine.
Among all mortal measures, the *tarantella* is as-
suredly the most delirious one, the most instinct
with motion and spirit, accumulating with a sort of
frantic and fierce earnestness that one might fancy
to be at variance with the light-heartedness of
mirth, did one not see it pervade every Italian
pursuit and pastime.   There is no playing or
dancing a *tarantella* sluggishly.   There may be
such things as a flaccid waltz and a heavy *galoppe*,
but the southern dance constrains all concerned in
its execution to a vivacity of animation to which no
parallel can be found, unless it be in the reel of
Scotland.

It is interesting to recollect how almost every
learned or fanciful musician has, at some time or
other, been enthralled by this whirling melody.
The grave Bach, the melancholy Chopin, the
sensuous Rossini, and half a hundred composers of
every mood and every colour, have all tried their
hands at *tarantella* making—almost all with great
success.   One of the most admirable examples of its
adoption is that made by Mendelssohn in the last

movement of his Symphony in A major, by some called the Italian Symphony.

The Russian dance employed with such vigour and brilliancy by Beethoven in the *finale* to his Symphony in A major, does not offer a more felicitous example of a composer seizing a national humour and turning it to account. Observe—for it is worth noting—that like the *Siciliana* and other dances, the *Coranto* and *Passacaglia*, which have tempted composers, this is in triple time. I think then, that this may be taken as a rule, with Italian popular melody : the newest example of it, perhaps, being the sickly *Santa Lucia*, which was but yesterday the favourite ditty of Naples—not to be escaped from by the travellers on their arrival in the bay, while wearily waiting until paternal government should have counted their numbers and called their names, and set them free to go ashore—or by the pilgrim when issuing from the City of the Dead, Pompeii.

I have a collection of the commonest street ditties, which I picked off the wall of a church in Naples, where they hung in fifties—purchased for an English shilling or thereabouts ; and one and all of these are in the *Barcarole* or *Brindisi* measure : to make an arbitrary use of familiar words. Here, however, is one which is somewhat odd, from an episodical phase of three bars which disturbs the symmetry of the rhythm.

tempo.

I have offered this specimen because of its irregularity; observing nevertheless, that though the
same is duly printed, the odd bar may be a case
of intentional caprice, which has perverted a commonplace melody.

Some years ago, when I was in Padua, while
resting my mind on the steps of Giotto's chapel,
after having looked at his noble frescoes there, I
was amused by listening to a girl who was arranging linen to dry under the mulberry trees, and
who sang a song of many verses to a ditty regular
and commonplace in every respect, save that the
third line was a five-bar phrase, which necessitated
the repetition of a word.

The oddity of the effect made me note the tune down : when I had done so, I called the singer to me, and asked her to sing the tune. This she did once, twice, thrice—always omitting the superfluous bar. I then sang it *to her*, as I had noted it, and as she had sung it to herself, and asked her which of the two versions was right. ' Why, the second one,' she said ; ' but *it amuses me to sing it thus* [with the five bars] *when I am by myself.*'

And if we go to Venice, we shall find the same predilection for a triple rhythm : as for instance, in the well-worn *Carnaval*.

I think I hear now a poor little grizzled creature, old enough to have seen something of better and gayer days in Venice, who, when I was there some twelve years ago, used to solace himself by piping out as he sculled along, or sat waiting on his steps for the passengers who rarely patronised him, a legend of the Virgin, which seemed to have no beginning or end, to a slow version of the waltz movement closing the lovely concerted piece, ' O guardate,' from Signor Rossini's ' Turco in Italia.'

There were a good many accidental flats and sharps added to this, probably resulting from the singer's extreme age and hunger; but the perpetual murmuring of the same travestied and trivial melody seemed to comfort him.

I may assume, then, that the triple rhythm is predominant throughout such national music of Italy, north or south, as is not scenic. For look among the chamber music of its best national composers. When the thing is not to be an opera scene, they seem by some unexplained instinct to fall into the form of three notes or bars, as the French do into the more active tramp of a four-in-a-bar or two-in-a-bar rhythm.

In Signor Rossini's exquisite chamber compositions, the same undulating movement prevails; and so again, it predominates in the canzonets of Signor Gordigiani, the last Italian composer who may be said to have produced something original.

For marked predilections like these there is no accounting. As little can it be explained why, seeing that the Italians were foremost in the manufacture of instruments, and are admirably skilled as players, instrumental composition, save in the most showy form of solitary display, should have fallen into such disesteem. In the concert-room, whether the arena be a theatre, or the Place of St. Mark's, or

a street in Genoa, or a riverside in Florence, while
the traveller is struck again and again with taught
and untaught proficiency on the part of the players,
he will hear nothing but some eternal song, or some
paltry dance, in nine cases out of ten from the
favourite opera.

For men of grave musical tendencies, such as
Clementi, and Cherubini, and Spontini, there has
been no home, no field for action in their own
country, for years and years past.

Such are a very few among the characteristics
of national music in Italy.   Perhaps, if followed
out, they might in some degree explain its reserves,
its past strength, its present weakness.

We have now to exchange the world of sentiment for that of intellectual vivacity, and to enter
a region of art originally colonised from the South,
no doubt, and of late time drawing tribute from every
country of the earth, with a self-consistency and
self-possession in which are involved nothing short
of absolute egotism and absolute metamorphosis.

For there is nothing more constant and tyran-
nical than certain characteristics of French art.   I
have outlined two, in reference to my subject: a
strangely assorted couple, but which arise and recur,

whatever field of inventive or imaginative enterprise be explored—monotony and piquancy.

Let me illustrate for a moment from French art in other forms than that of music.

To begin with drama : there is nothing so monotonous as all the rules of serious French tragedy—nothing so *piquant*, so provocative of intellectual curiosity, as the working-out of the same, by those who have to present it. Consider the *tirades* of Corneille and his successors, which, grand as they are, are rhymed—in a rhyme neither to be broken nor bent.

Yet tradition tells us in what measure Clairon,—and memory reminds my predecessors how Talma,—and personal experience has acquainted me by what sinister insinuations Rachel, *pointed* such monotony by a lacerating finesse of *accent* sufficient to carry off the platitude of the verse, and its deficiency in idea, and to support the situation of the scene.

I have found the same union of the same two separate elements in French painting. While the artists have shrunk from no subject, the similarity of expression in their elder pictures has always struck me. Till such romanticists as Gericault

with his 'Medusa Raft,' and Delaroche with his
'Murder of the Duke de Guise,' and Ary Scheffer
(who, by the way, was not French) appeared, there
was a curious repetition of the same set face to be
seen in their pictures; the same composed, man-
nered mouth, in the grand conventual compositions
of Philippe de Champagne, and in the Court portraits of Mignard, Rigaud, down even to Boucher.

In the architecture of the French the same
humour is to be traced. There is a peak (or *tourelle*)
on nine out of ten flat-bodied *chateaux*. Even in
such specimens as the Palace of the Tuileries, the
old portion of Fontainebleau, the chateau of Vallery,
near Sens, where the Great Condé lies buried (designed by Philibert de L'Orme), the monotony of the
line is relieved by piquancies in roof and chimney,
one setting off the other. I am persuaded that this
fancy, as pervading French art, will bear any amount
of illustration. But, to come to my own subject, the
peculiarity takes in music the form of a dry, limited
melody as applied to the setting of words, accompanied by a determination on the part of the executants in time, tone, and accent, to hold fast attention with both, or if not, then to snatch the ear
by disappointment and suspense. This definition

applies to their serious as well as to their comic
music; to the psalmodic recitations, relieved by
sharply cut dancing airs, in their grand or serious
operas, to the sprightly tunes of their *Vaudevilles*,
so often and again set off by a drone or pedal bass.
In brief, though the *esprit* of French music, old or
new, cannot *fascinate* any one, except he be a Frenchman born, it gives most active occupation to the
intellect that would appreciate, to the curiosity that
is in quest of individuality. It has by this power of
attraction drawn within its circle, and imposed laws
on artists belonging to all countries renowned in
connection with our art. From the days when opera
formed itself; when Lulli (to whom, by the way,
the well-known melody 'Au clair de la lune' is at-
tributed) was writing for Louis the Fourteenth; when
Mouret was making diversions for the country palace
of the Duchess of Maine; when Campra was surreptitiously creeping away from his church organ in
order to try his fortune on the stage; and when the
comic opera, the 'Théâtre de la Foire,' took its
shape, precursor of the *Vaudeville*—the dismal
regularity of what stood in stead of melody remained long a constant quality. Even Mendelssohn,
the last of the great Germans, put himself into

French dress when composing the choruses for Racine's 'Athalie.'

Further, as consistent with the above theory, there has never been such a nation of song-singers as the French, beginning with the troubadour days of romance, and going on to the later times, when the lay of 'The Armed Man' went through Europe as a ditty, in such favour that fifty Italian masses were based on it—I presume, on Rowland Hill's well-known principle. Dreary must have been the notions of melody that could accept such a theme. The charm must have lain in the tale of chivalry or adventure recited ; in the warlike feats of Roland, or in the pica-roon exploits of 'Count Ory.' Nevertheless, it cannot have been altogether the import of the words which contented the listeners. That they must have taken a real pleasure in monotonous and prosy tunes is evi-dent, since the Geneva hymns to the Psalms of David, translated by Clement Marot, were popular among the ladies and gentlemen of not the most devout court in Europe.

But, however persevering as singers of words the French have been, their natural endowments as vocalists appear to have been always singular and restricted.

The men of France are largely to be distinguished by a mixed voice, neither conscientiously tenor nor honestly bass. This will be seen by their operas: those of Gluck, for instance, are so written as to be very difficult of execution to the bass singers of other countries.

Such men in comic opera were Calliot, whom Burney describes; Martin;—in our own day, Chollet, for whom Herold's ' Zampa ' was written.

Then, again, in France will largely be found the high male counter-tenor organ, which justified the sarcasm, ' *That or the other nose has a good voice,*' whereas the low female or contralto voice has been always rare; I cannot recollect a solitary French example. So much for peculiarities of register: generally, the quality of vocal tone, take it in what scale you will, is inferior, harsh, poor, not winning; nor can this wholly lie on the difficulties of the language. The close vowels of France are not so directly opposed to amenity of sound as the guttural consonants of Germany and the sibilants of England.

The French appreciation of suavity of tone, moreover, may be described as having kept pace with the supply. The lady who, as a stage widow in a wreath of black flowers, screamed so at the grand opera as to shock Horace Walpole,—the Madame Laïs, whom Moore, I think, signalised in his 'Fudge Family' for like ear-piercing qualities, were long the types of French singers who entirely contented their public, and were commemorated by the wits and epigram writers—not as so many muses, but as so many nightingales. In old Italian scores, when the singer was to force out one of those violences to which Signor Verdi has hardened southern ears, the direction was '*un nolo Francese*,' a French scream. Times have changed with the singers of France.

These peculiarities cannot but have imparted a certain tone and cast to French melody on the one hand, while on the other the *esprit* rather than the fancy of the poets has encouraged in it turns, surprises, in which quaint and modish cleverness is more remarkable than natural beauty. And this not without grace, inasmuch as Watteau is graceful. There must be a corner kept for the world of revels at the *Trianon*, as well as for those in the *Corso*, by all who are not bowed, and braced and barred by their own narrowness into one form of Art.

The excellent manner in which these national peculiarities have been turned to account by the composers of France, must strike every one familiar with their music.

Successively such remarkable men as Rameau, Boieldieu, Herold, Auber, and Halevy, while availing themselves of every contemporary discovery with great readiness, have, either from instinct or predilection, kept close to the style of their country.

You will rarely meet with a slow movement by them which possesses that relishing or sweet freshness that belongs to similar German or Italian specimens by men of merit.

You will as rarely come on a sprightly measure in which some unforeseen turn of interval or rhythm does not redeem the tune from commonplace, if even at the price of added affectation.

This fact will repay the most minute examination by the student of melody—a branch of musical education, let me say, which is far too largely neglected. It is far too much forgotten, that a touch judiciously applied, a note withdrawn or changed, may transform that which is valueless into that which is attractive—a barren phrase into a suggestive idea.

The above, which is from M. Auber's 'Lac des Fées,' is a veritable type of French taste in melody, and affords a peep into such French fairyland as Watteau might have painted. It is worth comparing with the fairy music written by Mendelssohn for our 'Midsummer Night's Dream.'

Once more—to be monotonous, in reverting to French monotony—this characteristic may have been to some degree as much encouraged by the instrumental predilections of the French, as by the peculiarity of their voices. The national instrument has a drone, whether it be the *vielle*, or hurdy-gurdy, or the bagpipe—that primitive walking-organ, for which I have confessed a secret affection, utterly heterodox though it be. Madame George Sand, who has a keen musical sense and some understanding, assures us that in the central provinces of France many brave pipers are to be found, taught by ear and imitation, who can name neither clef nor note, but who catch up, who vary and invent tunes with great adroitness; and it is certain that throughout the music of no country is so much of the *musette* or drone bass to be heard, as in the music of France.

The first specimen I shall offer is an old ' *Brunette*,' or love ditty; the dark complexion, it has been said, (in explanation of the term) being in such favour, as to represent the every-day *Cynthia* whom the every-day *Cymon* of the regulated pastoral was to court, or else to complain of. There are hundreds of tunes of this kind, belonging to the same period, the seventeenth century.

Allegro Moderato.

In the following—which is the beginning of
an *arietta* with chorus and dance, from 'Hyppolite
et Aricie,' the first opera of Rameau, who was the
first national composer of genius that could be
named—the same drone is applied to a different
rhythm, with more art and science. I know
nothing contemporaneous, either in Italian or

German music, at once so monotonous and piquant as this.

As we draw towards our own time, examples multiply by the thousand: to be found, for instance, in Boieldieu's overture to 'The Caliph of Bagdad,' or Berton's to 'Aline,' by scores in the operas of M. Auber. To conclude this train of speculation, I cannot do better than cite an example of monotony and piquancy, in their most graceful and exquisite union, from 'L'Ambassadrice,' by M. Auber, the patriarch of modern French composers.

The newest French composer to whom, in default of more real genius, Europe is beginning to look for its operas—I mean M. Gounod—is employing the same device with a felicity, but also with a pertinacity, which proves how deeply the spirit thereof is ingrained into the body of French music.

Enough has been said of the pipers and their drone; but, from the two, we are naturally led on to the dancers; and these have formed always an important part of the people of France. Indeed, I believe there might be some fossil men and women quarried

I

out of remote places in England, who still think of the French as mainly a nation of dancing-masters.

In the dances of the French there will be found vivacities of measure as curious as the solemnity of *Cantilena* in their serious song.

The melodies of Auvergne, arrangéd by Onslow, our countryman, naturalised there, are doleful enough; but from Auvergne we get that dance, the *Bourré*: a brisk rustic measure which has prompted great composers, and established a *tempo* in music. Many of Handel's songs are written in *Tempo de Bourré*. I may instance the charming one in 'Joshua,' 'Heroes when with glory burning,' and in 'Jephtha,' the delicious first song of Jephtha's daughter, 'The smiling dawn of happier days.' Bach, again, who had a hankering after every foreign style, though he was a man who lived and died among his own people—the most German of Germans—employed the measure bravely.

Other dances may be named as characteristic of France—the *Braule,* or 'Brawl'—which, it may be recollected, Marie Stuart is said to have led at the wedding of her servant Sebastian, on the night of Darnley's murder—a stately tune in three-four time, resembling the *Passacaille* and the *Pavane*—and the

Ronde, which is again in common metre. This rhythm, I think, may be described as the one most congenial to French sympathies.

Their *Gavotte* is close to the minuet, of such elegant gaiety as to deserve expressly complimentary mention. And where in the world is there anything like the mad sweep of the *Galoppe*!—a dance which it is almost hopeless to attempt anywhere out of France—with all its stream of smooth yet rapid craziness; as unapproachable in its character by the natives of other countries as were the charming floating graces of the three-bar waltz of Germany—ere the modern, and, I think, senseless dislocation of it was invented by Folly, spoiling a good and genuine thing as completely as if (to use a quaint phrase of Dr. Franklin's) you put ' salt to strawberries.'

To the rich wit of the French (who nevertheless are poor in the sense of the whimsical) must be ascribed many of the forms of their music when used to mate sound with sense for stage uses, whether in the *Vaudeville*, or in the table-song, or in the *Amphigouri*, that sort of medley which has its equivalent in no other country.

For the most part, when the domain of French popular art has been entered, it will be perceived that, provided the tune has a certain piquancy, let it be 'common as a barber's chair'—to quote the author of 'Philip von Artevelde'—so that it only has a burden, no matter with what jargon, to which people can march, or make a noise in time, it is satisfying and delightful.

The pungency which the vocalist can *sting* into his words, the crispness of rhythm, are of greater consequence than beauty of voice or originality of melody.

I need only touch very slightly upon the admirable piquancy of the Comic Opera music of France, because the fact is as well confessed as was the supremacy of their cookery in the days before that great and serious art began to wane; and because I wish to dwell on the section of French tunes to which my characteristics apply *in their faintest manifestation*: I mean certain modern frank ditties of wine and war, of political satire or popular tumult.

Here, however, though the frankness is largely to be noted, the words are allowed to get the better of the music, and to impose on it certain peculiarities of rhythm.

I could fill a chapter, and perhaps not without bringing out some forgotten points, were I to attempt to enter on the tunes which spited Madame du Barri in the pride of her shameless ascendancy : ' La Belle Bourbonnaise ' being one of the most ferocious airs which later taunted and tormented Marie Antoinette. Though these political and patriotic songs have small musical value, the recurrence of one character in them is remarkable—a character more frank, more distinct, more vulgar (if you please), than in the case of any other French music.

To illustrate this, I will dwell for a moment on the best known one, ' La Marseillaise,' because of the controversy lately raised in respect to its parentage. A claim has been put forward from the Lake of Constance by inhabitants of that small village, Meersburg—with its palace on an insulated fragment of rock, not so very unlike a drum, and oddly jammed in between the hill and the lake.

Meersburg was, even so late as the close of the last century, an episcopal see, where state was held and music was encouraged; and on the strength of a manuscript that is existing there, we are instructed that ' La Marseillaise ' was not made, but borrowed, from a mass at Meersburg.

This might pass, so far as any belief in the integrity of its reputed author is concerned. For the author was Rouget de Lille : in talent, if

not in fortune, a sort of French Dibdin, who wrote
songs and composed music to them in an irregular
way of his own, but in which there was something
of art as well as of poetry : a man who was pitied
and assisted by Béranger, and who died in misery
and want.   His collection of fifty ' Songs of France '
is a rather sad comment on the elastic nature of his
patriotism, ranging as it does betwixt the years 1776
and 1821, and comprising all manner of hymns got
up for all manner of triumphant occasions—Repub-
lican, Imperial, and Legitimist.

'La Marseillaise,' purported to have been written,
words and music, at Strasbourg in the year 1792,
called originally the song of ' The Rhine Army ' by
the author, who seems to have been wandering in
want of bread, and re-christened after its appearance
in a journal of Marseilles—was by no means De Lille's
first essay. Now it is *possible* that the Meersburg mass
referred to may have been heard by him at Strasbourg, though hardly probable—seeing that then the
places were two days' journey apart : seeing that every
Catholic town had its affluence of small composers ;
and it is possible that he may have pillaged it of the
' Credo ' and twisted that hymn literally to his own
patriotic uses.

But it is more *probable* that the hymn may have got to Meersburg, since on the authentication of the manuscript I lay small stress, and for the following reasons :—

The style of the ' Marseillaise ' was clearly anticipated in other earlier songs by De Lille, unless these were misdated, or forgeries. The song of ' Roland ' by him, dated 1776—and if this be correct, composed when Rouget de Lille was sixteen, his birth year being 1760—has clearly the very precise form of sharp, keen, animated measure, marked by dotted notes and trumpet calls, to which people can tramp in time—and the French love to tramp, as any one acquainted with theatrical audiences must know—which was later made out with greater power in the ' Marseillaise.' Traces of this peculiar movement are constantly to be found in French music of a certain quality, even of late days. Everyone knows the melody ' Brulant d'Amour : "

as one among twenties—shall I not say, hundreds ?—

analogous to which, I can only recall few from beyond
the frontier—such, for example, as Lindpaintner's
'Standard Bearer,' which Herr Pischek brought to
England.

Now, I repeat, this matter of style is a stubborn
stumbling-block to those who have studied it. What
availed the denials of Scott, when he was taxed with
his novels? Simply to make the 'dropping of the
mask' a not very graceful proceeding.

A James Smith can manage a page of mimicry
in his 'Rejected Addresses' which shall seem reality,
but cannot keep it up for a lifetime. If this
'Credo' of the Meersburg Mass was the inspiration
of Rouget de Lille, it must been so by a sort of
prevision which tinctured many of his earlier compositions; and the rhythm of the tune, in which lies
its character, the few modulations being of the commonest quality, must have struck a deeper root in
France than a form derived from a composition born
in so obscure a quarter was likely to do. The case

is one in which I cannot fancy evidence standing
against inference.

In retaliation on our German cousins, it may be
pointed out that they have listened to the 'Marseillaise' to good purpose, since this phrase perpetually occurs in their student and wine songs:

Which is virtually identical with the fourth line of
the 'Marseillaise,' leaving out the spirit of the dotted
quavers:

If the Germans have desired to get the credit of
the 'Marseillaise' from the French, our allies have
attempted a still more heinous usurpation, having
laid claim to nothing less national than our National
Hymn, which they have maintained was the composition of Lulli, their adopted musician. During
the seventeenth and eighteenth centuries, in England
and elsewhere (as Mr. William Chappell's carefully
executed collection attests), a pompous minuet style
was in fashion, some twenty specimens of which
bear as close a family likeness one to the other as
Rouget de Lille's military tunes.

Here is a specimen by Lulli: a minuet movement
preluding an *ariette* from a ballet by him, 'La Mas-
carade de Versailles.'

From the midst of many tunes in this form I conceive that our National Hymn combined itself, rather than was composed; the difficulties in admission of the French claim lying in the fact that the rhythm of the verse—two lines with a burden, followed by three lines with a burden—is only, so far as I know, found in our language. There is, however, a certain analogous irregularity in 'Charmant Gabrielle,' where a six-bar phrase, twice repeated, is followed by a five-bar one, also reiterated. Books have been published on the matter; but on the extreme caution with which I conceive tradition should be accepted, when at variance with conviction resulting from comparison, I have no need to dwell.

I regret to be compelled to deny myself the indulgence of further speculations on the peculiar qualities of French music; earnestly calling attention to it as a subject *far too much slighted*, and, whether it be viewed in connection with manners, with other arts, or with other nationalities, a subject full of matter, curious, interesting, and replete with instruction.

MUSIC FROM THE NORTH.

I DEALT in the last essay with national music which may have derived much of its colour, as in Italy, from emotion— as in France, from the intellectual predilections of the people.

The domain to be now entered is one largely pervaded by the *fantastic* element.

In lands of mists and of mountains—of long winters, and summers all the more precious because they are so short, days of grace snatched out of a dark year—the influences of scenery are more clearly to be discerned than in regions where nature is more uniformly favourable. Be the national music of the North natural or gay, it is for the most part fresh. The sadness of it is seldom tinctured with languor; the sweetness has something in it that braces as well as that charms the sense.

This even may be remarked when the minor key predominates so largely, as in the tunes of the districts to which I shall first advert.

On the subject of keys, it may be asked, if we have not unreasonably cherished fancies arising from peculiarities in executive power, rather than any intrinsic gravity or gaiety of sound. Every musician's ear has its own predilections, as has every painter's eye for a peculiar colour. The Mozart progression, the Rossini close—so cleverly compared by Liszt to the signature, ' *Yours truly,*' which finishes a letter—the Mendelssohn chords, are as distinctive of their owners as Domenichino's marigold yellow, or Cenerino's ash-grey, in the pictures of those masters. I have dared to entertain a heresy, that the setting of a particular tone in its place is of as much consequence as its intrinsic quality ; and that the wholesale definitions of sharps as brilliant, and of flats as melancholy, have been traded on to an extremity.

To offer a simple illustration.

In these days of ours, every composer who attempts a funeral march thinks it necessary to pile flat upon flat in the minor key, because Beethoven did so in the march from the well-known Sonata, Opus 26, and in the still more solemn example (yet less flat by four flats) from his ' Eroica ' symphony. Now, somehow, our great old Handel outdid these magnificent compositions, with his crude orchestra, in his two Dead Marches—those, I mean, from 'Saul' and 'Samson.' The first of these is in C major (which used to be called the 'wanton key'), and the second is in D major. I cannot fancy the simple and noble pathos of these exceeded.

I may draw another illustration from such works of greater length as operas, where many keys are used in succession and alternation. Now hearing, as we have done so much of late, that the diapason during the past century has been raised half a tone, it would follow, that had keys much intrinsic value beyond that of the player's or singer's convenience, bright must have become dark, and *vice versâ*.

In all these preferences, I repeat, personality is mixed up largely. I remember hearing six ingenious musicians laying their heads together to agree that no grave music had been ever written in the key of G major. The pleasant flow of their concord was interrupted by a seventh speaker, who quietly cited 'See the Conquering Hero comes,' and the chorus from the 'Messiah,' 'For unto us a Child is born,' not to speak of Haydn's 'God preserve the Emperor.'

These crotchets, my own speculations counting in the list, will always have a great attraction for persons who are decided in their likes or dislikes, but for the moment the matter must here be left.

It is impossible to overrate the freshness and vigour of the song-melody of the north—*let the key be what it will.* These bear company with like qualities in the popular poetry. And though trained art taking any form of originality is comparatively modern in the North, as compared with the South, the tunes themselves have a quaint sharpness of interval and rhythm, which amounts to a charac-teristic.

I must now enter into a detail or two. To begin with Muscovy. Russian music has singular par-ticularities; among these, the double-bass voices—ranging, I believe, from about D in the bass stave to D below the line—who support the chords of the chants of the national worship.

I am unable to speak of the effect of this chant-ing, save from the exhibition of it on a very reduced scale, which is to be met with in Paris. Even that, simple and monotonous as the music is, is most impressive; from its sweetness of tone, surety of intonation, and certainty of attack.

Witnesses to be relied on assure us that, as heard in the great Churches of St. Petersburg and Moscow, executed by a mass of finer voices than any permitted to travel abroad, the impression of this Russian sacred music in its sublimity exceeds even that of the more accessible Easter music at Rome, concerning which so much has been written. I had long an idea, that the music of the Russian church might be influenced by Greek traditions; that its chants might be the old chants: but, so far as I can understand, the singularity of interval which distinguishes the old Ambrosian or Gregorian tune, does not pervade the *cantilena* or melody—and the whole music of the rite is a modernised music. On this matter, which however I have taken some pains to ascertain, I can only speak from hearsay, not inspection of manuscripts.

Physical effects like these adverted to, from the double-bass voices, can only be obtained under the conditions of serfdom; since the singers can be little more than machines, comprising each a few select notes, whose owners are fit for small other service.

The perfection derived from limitation or division of labour such as this, when applied to art, can only be obtained when society is primitive—as in India, where there is one functionary to bridle a horse, and another to put on his saddle; where one man will sit on his seat to stitch the coming baby's cap, while the man whose duty is grown-up embroidery addicts himself to the lady mother's robe of state. *Caste,* in national music, is a thing which has never been studied aright, so far as I am aware. Stranger than these double-bass voices, but akin in their training, seem to have been—or perhaps yet are—the players on the horn-bands of Russia; automatons of one note, referable again to the state of serfdom; of no more real value or sentiment in regard to art than so many organ pipes—than so many pins which decide the A, B, or C, ground out of the barrel of the hand-organ.

Those who care to follow the subject may measure these strange machines with a home-set of popular musicians, and who are somewhat mechanical also—our bell-ringers: each of whom, also, has only one note to care for. But bell-ringing, besides its being a hearty and voluntary exercise for the athletic, has something of variety and unexpectedness in its changes—an appeal in them to calculation as well as to recollection, which the playing of these Russian monotones has not.

The Russian voice, however, be it free or slave,

is universally allowed to be most melodious. It would be impossible in quality to outvie that of a singer whom many living recollect—Signor Ivanoff.

As to the Russian melodies, I shall select *three*. The first, I cannot but conceive has been arranged, but there is in it a character well worth considering.

The second is a sort of wicked dance (if rightly noted), to which no innocent person—I mean regardful of responsibility in step and 'hands across and back again'—*could* dance.

The third, which from the rude printing of the text I conceive may be the most genuine, is capital, because of the three-bar phrases.

Some of these Russian tunes were excellently wrought on by Beethoven in his variations, in his Razoumouffsky Quartetts; other Northern tunes, by his pupil Ferdinand Ries: a composer who has been too much forgotten, perhaps, because he was Beethoven's pupil, but whose best works do not belong to Beethoven.

I must now take a glimpse at other northern districts, which have proved themselves abundant in materials of art; and not merely so, but as yielding products bearing a certain family likeness one to other—products that suggest the idea of

snow statues—of Aurora Borealis—of Eolian harp—
of Shakspeare's 'Ophelia'—of everything that is cold,
whimsical, quaint, and elfish, yet not inexpressive.
Let me name such a group of artists as Thorwaldsen,
Madame Taglioni, Herr Andersen, Madame Lind-
Goldschmidt, and Herr Gade,—all artists belonging
to the far land of mist and snow.

The Swedes are eminently a musical people. One
of their old sea-laws, I am told by a Swede, was that
a hymn by the man on the watch, at sea, should be
sung every night. Surely there is something truly
picturesque, as well as devout, in such an ordinance.
I announced at the outset, that I was not intending
to adduce any great beauty of illustration, but I am
about to do so. I cannot warrant the date of the
following tune, but it comes from a collection which
appears to be conscientiously prepared, and the airs
in it to be exactly noted.

SWEDISH AIR.

In the above wild air there is a suggestion of the wandering sweetness which is to be found in the songs of Lindblad, the individuality of which is equalled only by their charm. Though they bear the form of the German *lied*, they have not the least of the German character, such as will be found expressed in the *lieder* of Schubert, Mendelssohn, and Schumann.

Then, the far Northern folk have brave dancing measures of their own.

Their *Polska*—not the weed from which the *Polka* has grown (because that dance was invented by a servant girl not very long ago), so much as a corruption, it may be fancied, of Polonoise—is a brisk marked time, with humours of its own. What follows has been *glossed*, obviously, by some country fiddler : one of those players whose magical power in inspiriting their dancers is so picturesquely described in 'Strife and Peace,' that pleasant northern novel by Miss Bremer. She tells us, by the way, that the fiddle played on is not a common one, but, so far as can be made out from her description, has four metallic strings under the sounding-board, as well as the usual catgut four, the vibration of which under strings produces a most peculiar effect.

It is curious to observe the similarity of style *in decoration* among the national players of every country; how perpetually they attempt to disguise imperfect execution by little conventional turns, and trills, and tricks, and by an odd employment of the *appoggiatura*. The graces of the guitar

players of Spain, of the **harpers of Ireland,** of the
gipsy-folk from Bohemia, and of those who in the
far North set the young people dancing, bear a strange
family likeness one to the other. The same characteristics are apparent in the Danish airs, combined
into a march by Mr. Arthur Sullivan, which were
played before a Danish lady, our Princess, on the
day when *by storm*—no, by *charm*—she entered our
city, and conquered London.

And next—since, in a subject so wide, grouping
becomes indispensable—let me call attention to the
fact that all mountain pastoral music has a character of its own, as clearly defined as the Sicilian
style lately considered. In the herdsmen's songs of
Norway, in the foresters' tunes of the Tyrol, in
the melodies of Switzerland, the hill echo and the
simple mountain horn are to be heard without fail.
How charmingly these fall on the ear, need not
be told; whether they be met in their primitive
simplicity in some delicious summer evening scene,
of pass or lake, or quaint wooden village, or in-
spiring some jolly German part-song, or when
wrought into such an exquisite tissue as Signor
Rossini's ' Guillaume Tell.'

These mountain tunes have been more largely

used in what may be called civilised music than
any other wild vocal melodies: not merely from
their intrinsic freshness, but because they are
minutely susceptible of harmonic treatment. In
fact, among the Tyrolese especially, they largely
take the form of part-songs: the peasantry, without
having learned counterpoint, instinctively putting
together those few and simple chords which, though
sometimes incorrect, are always effective. The character of this hill music is too marked, however, in
the recurrence of certain intervals —

for it to bear any harmonic intricacy or torture.

Here is one which has been treated by Beethoven,
among his easy variations, for piano and violin, of
popular tunes. I fancy it little known.

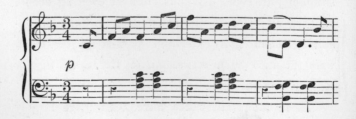

The *zither*, something betwixt a dulcimer and guitar, plays an animated part in the Tyrolese music. The sounds whipped out of its metallic chords are stinging and brilliant, and especially in the open air, where all catgut strings lose resonance, prove most effective as supporting the voices.

The national music of *Poland*, matured into complete art at a period far earlier than any corresponding transformation in Russia, would furnish full matter for a chapter by itself.

The organisation of the people—the same which makes them so remarkable as linguists—more picturesque, subtle, and flexible, perhaps, than *genial*, singularly lent itself to the cultivation of music.

The courts of Poland were liberal and pompous in its encouragement from an early period; the nobles munificent in patronage; the Church, as everywhere else, eager to appropriate its services.

The Pope of Rome was without his hymn till
the other day: the guardian saints, Casimir and
Adalbert, were centuries before him; the former in
particular having been fitted with a tune by Dio-
medes the composer, a naturalised Venetian attached
to the court of Sigismund III., of which the regularity and stateliness are remarkable, considering
its date, 1607.

In 1647, when the king of Poland visited the convent of our lady of Czenstochowa, and was received with the thunder of cannon and of bells, an ancient Polish canticle was executed, the regularity of which recalls the well-known hymn, 'Alla Trinita.'

M. Sowinski, to whose biographical dictionary, ill-executed as it is, I am indebted for these details, cites a Christmas Carol of still earlier date, which is curious. If the Italians got their sacred cradle music from the Sicilian pastoral, the Poles may have got their mazurka measure from the old Christmas tune.

It will be seen that the measure is the one improved by Chopin, whose mazurkas made, as did Mendelssohn's 'Songs without Words,' a new appearance in music.

But I must remind the reader of my mistrust of tradition : and all the more here than in any other section of my subject, because the Poles, as a nation, are rather exacting in their demands on belief.

I heard some years ago, in Paris, one of the most distinguished amateurs of their or of any other country scold himself hoarse, in his resolution to maintain that the greater number of the subjects in Mozart's 'Don Giovanni' were Polish melodies.

The Poles had every sort of instrument, and great musical schools, less largely fed by assistance from Italy than any contemporaries of which traces are to be found. Of late, they have sent out players on certain instruments, the violin and pianoforte, to every corner of the earth: such as Duranowski, who is said to have suggested his effects to Paganini, and Lipinski, just dead; and not merely men of such high standing, but a host of trained executants ready for subordinate occupation. M. Sowinski, in his book, mentions that so lately as 1833-34 there was a large and rich military band at Bourges, in France, entirely composed of exiled Poles. If they have been less eminent as vocal writers and composers, the fault may have lain in their language, which, with its heaps of consonants—the letter *z* being especially prominent—outvies in every line of their verse the exceptional names satirically introduced by Milton into his well-known 'Tetrachordon' sonnet.

Then there is the National Music of Bohemia, with a distinct character of its own, and an original power which has engraven deep traces on the works of what may be called cultivated artists. The extent and reality of this have been overlooked, because the district is one sparingly visited by tourists, though it would well bear being ransacked. The farmers and rural folk, who live about among the hills, we are assured by those who know the recesses of the country, have long had a heritage of musical capacity, and for a century past, at least, considerable training among themselves and in their village schools ; by which an average instrumental proficiency more than respectable has been obtained. From serving the purposes of village festivals, sacred and secular, they were drawn gradually into the sphere of outward notice by the resort to watering places, which during the last century began to be an indulgence, and has since grown into an epidemic.

These men have long largely furnished forth the military bands and the dance orchestras of southern Germany, on the strength of nothing more than such teaching as has been described, during the long winter evening hours to be beguiled in an inhospitable climate. I shall not engage the sympathy of some of my readers, by saying that what may be called the off-scourings of these districts find their way largely into foreign countries, and into the London streets. The best have risen ; some, of themselves, separating themselves from their old haunts and habits, while others have embellished the one and turned the other to account. I may name as a type of the latter class, Labitsky : a man of humble origin, but who rose to very great proficiency as an instrumental player, and whose dance-music has a European reputation beside that of Strauss and Lanner. I am assured by those who should know, that the themes of many of the waltzes so effectively arranged and combined by him are national tunes. It is to be observed that the harp plays an important part in the Bohemian music touched on, one of Tubal Cain's two primitive instruments, the organ, being the other.

My attention was drawn to this subject by a most interesting monograph, by Dr. Marnel, of Carlsbad, published in a local journal of the place many years ago : one of the many scattered productions which, because of their form, are too apt to be overlooked and forgotten ; the collection of which would be of important value to the historian and philosopher who studies music in connection with climates, customs, and forms of society.

The South German waltz is one of the most characteristic musical possessions of South Germany ; perhaps the only one concerning which critics and connoisseurs of all creeds, races, and dialects, are agreed: in its slow and sentimental form tempting every composer, be he ever so disdainful of trifling, and in this guise displaying the most exquisite melodies of a land not very rich in vocal melody; in its own rapid and practical existence calling out an amount of ingenuity, air, grace, and variety, which entirely conceal the narrowness of the limits within which they move. In no desire to misrepresent a trifle as a treasure, but in consistency with my former speculations on dance music, do I call attention to the Austrian waltzes, as to one of the most unique sections of the world of music. The flowing melody is rarely vulgar; the tunes are many of them derived from other than German sources—French, Italian, Scotch, and what not. But they were so transformed, so varied, by happy accidents and suspenses of rhythm—by natural yet piquant successions of key to key—in the hands of such men as those who have been named, that they have gained a life, a reality, a pertinence of their own, which no foreigner can reach. The tunes worked on by Strauss were other people's tunes, but he made them new, as gold can be made new, whether it be worked into a bar, or a trifle for a lady's chamber.

I do not recollect one respectable Italian waltz. The two which Signor Verdi has attempted in his operas are the most paltry of the paltry; and Signor Rossini's 'Guillaume Tell,' which contains a capital specimen of a waltz as sequel to a quick step, cannot be considered as an Italian opera. There is one excellent French specimen, by M. Gounod, but this is in the 'Fair-scene' from his 'Faust'—a proof how admirably he has caught up the character and colour of his subject; a tune for which I would give libraries of 'concealed melody,' (we have absolutely lived to hear of such a curiosity,) and of the doleful settings of dreamy words which have come to pass with our neighbours for songs. But this is the only essay in the waltz style by a Frenchman, which I remember as sufferable. Adam, a composer who had a taste for colour; Musard, who as managing a *galoppe* was as national as Strauss, and as inimitable, could make nothing of the rhythm. The South Germans are born waltzers, and the Northerns, not unwilling, are bred ones.

Space permits me to go no further in the separate specification of the threads (so to say), all of which, however, lying apart as they do, and belonging to widely different races, dialects, and sympathies—are

still woven into the web of German, as distinguished
from Italian music.

Many German men of great name were cradled
among these primitive melodies. Every one among
them has been far more largely indebted to the popular
element than were the great men of Italy in *their*
generation. Yet the music of German art, in which
science expressed the national spirit, had to endure a
hard birth-struggle ere it could be born and perfected.
So far beforehand was Italy in the secrets of knowledge
and form, so rich then in artists whom she could spare
to Germany, so widely have her fascinations always
pervaded Europe, that foreign influences and prepos-
sessions were in every Court and tinctured every
fountain of honour for many years. Some of the best
of the German men of genius Italianized themselves, such as Handel; such as the Bohemian composer, called in Italy Il Boemo; such as Hasse, from
Saxony, and others.

Precisely the converse of the course of art in
Italy has been that of German music. In the South,
noble and courtly patronage and *participation* did
much—in the North, little; because, although there
were such amateurs as a Great Frederick of
Prussia, and a Saxon Electress who composed operas,

these, like other royalties, affected the foreign style, and until a very recent period recognised no other. True, they opened their courts to great musicians, but those of home-growth often met with strange entertainment—apart from the stipend, which sometimes placed them in easy circumstances. I need not recall the struggles of Mozart to get something better than a lackey's pay and a lackey's treatment out of the Prince Archbishop of Salzburg, nor the total neglect which darkened Beethoven's latter days in Vienna; how Spohr, after he was a European celebrity, when admitted to play at a certain Court, had to work hard to get a thick carpet taken up, which had been laid down expressly to make the music of the household band as inoffensive as possible, in order that the card-players, to whom the music was an accompaniment, might not be disturbed; how the pianoforte music of Weber (that most national of German composers, as we shall presently see), was exhibited at the Court of Saxony to the jingle of knives and forks, while the Court was at dinner. The musician was decorated with orders and endowed with maintenance; but whereas in Italy he was in some sort an equal, in Germany he was, after all, but a vassal, and this till within a late period.

We have seen in Russia how serfdom aided music of combination in the church and in the palace. Reasoning from analogy, I am compelled to admit the fancy that this vassalage, or state of dependence, may have had something to do in giving German music one of its most distinctive features—that orchestral perfection which depends alike on sympathy and on discipline.

It may not only have been such adaptability as makes English sailors pre-eminent—such peculiarity of organisation as makes Irish singers bad timists, and French players so admirable in point of rhythm and accent, to which these dispositions for executing music of combination are to be ascribed; because, though German speech pervades a wide country, it is a country of many countries, peopled by many races. I thus cannot dismiss the fancy, that to the forms of a society in which despotism was not unaccompanied by encouragement, may be partly ascribed some of the forms of art, and partly the habits of life among those who, whether Northern or Southern, have too often fancied liberty to sanction unpunctuality, and sentiment as modifying sense of obligation.

But a germ of self-asserting nationality was in

the Germans, and there were simple and quiet masters of their art who stayed at home while they looked abroad, and matured their mighty inventions in the strength of their own individuality—such as Sebastian Bach, the greatest master of composition for a peculiar instrument, and the greatest performer on it whom the world has ever seen; a man whose invention was as untiring as his industry, but whose share of melody was smaller than his experimental ingenuity and science; and whose works, though a mass of solid and richly-finished treasure, in one section of them unparagoned, and as fresh to-day as on the day they were made, still indicate the organisation of one slenderly alive to vocal charm.

Almost contemporaneously with this manifestation of a peculiar bias towards instrumental composition in the North, that proclivity towards the fantastic, the descriptive and the mystical, showed itself, which has done so much to determine the bent of national genius. Even Bach, the grave fugue-writer, could, in anticipation of Beethoven's 'Adieu' sonata, make up a *fantasia* on the events of a journey, comprising the 'dissuasion of friends' and 'their representation of dangers to be expected,' the traveller's firmness, and the like.

An elder, a graver, and drier organist and composer than Bach, Buctehude of Lubeck, had composed a series of solemn pieces on the planets. All
these home tendencies, especially so soon as there be-
came any thought of marshalling them in antagonism
against foreign fantasies, told inevitably against that
ease, symmetry, and simplicity which are the life,
body, and soul of vocal writing.

Here, again, peculiarity of material must also be
taken into account. It may be said, without any lack
of charity, that the German language, save it be
managed with no ordinary delicacy and precision, is
not euphonious when sung. The German women
have naturally beautiful voices of first-rate *soprano*
quality; the *contralto* voice is as generically inferior.
The tenors are high, throaty, and forcible; the bass
voices deep, rich, and extensive. But no less certainly may it be averred, that the art of managing
the voice, so as to make it sing strenuously in
chorus, is misunderstood and undervalued among the
Germans. I remember the names of only three
soprani voices, largely indebted to northern training,
who have made an European reputation: Mara,
Sontag (who owed much to the influences of Madame
Fodor and Madame Pasta), and lastly, Madame

M

Goldschmidt; no tenor that could stand a moment's competition with the Italians; only one bass—I mean Staudigl.

There is a phrase of late current—'nature singing,' implying an insensibility, an inconsistency, or an ignorance; the negative weakness of which must sap the foundations of a lovely branch of art. There is a golden mean between soulless vocal display and the utter abnegation of accomplishment; but the national, northern-bred fancy for what is vague, mysterious, and suggestive, has too often invested those who affect the latter with some sublimity. They wear an aureole glory of mystical inspiration round their brow, which sets them apart from the common frivolous folk whose art gives a more artless pleasure.

I think some of the first distinct stirrings of German individuality may be referred to Luther's Psalm-Book. That genial man represented the legend of Orpheus, in his own bold Christian fashion, and besides assaulting the Evil One with his inkstand, defied, instead of paralysing him, by songs. But though 'psalm-singing' was on high authority appointed to be the pastime of the merry, sense, as well as spirit, will and *should* have its part in every scheme of human life. The poor scholars might sing chorals in the streets at the doors of the merchants; but the merchants' sons wanted something more jolly to sing over their pipes and their bottles of Rhine wine and Lubeck beer. Before an Elector of Saxony rejoiced in his Italian Opera company, brought from afar at a vast expense; and an Electress amused her amateurship by composing a 'Talestri,'[15] as a later Dresden Princess did plays; before a King of Prussia could at once Frenchify his theatre and dragoon it, as he dragooned his grenadiers, and indulge his amateurship by composing marches and playing three flute concertos every night; the merchants and tradesmen of Hamburgh had established an opera for themselves, and set up a composer of their own.

When the guilds began to get together, and the students to escape some very short steps from beyond the pedantic thraldom of the old notions— when the spirit of association began to possess itself of the young men, whether for purposes of craftsmanship or good-fellowship—then, gradually, a spirit began to manifest itself in the North in the form of the part-song for men.

---

[15] A 'serious drama' thus entitled.—ED.

Then this male part-singing was somewhat urged on the multitude by the position of the German woman, which generally, during the days when cultivated music was taking its national form, was not that of man's companion, so much as of his slave : tenderly treated—honoured, it may be—but not associated in all his pleasures, as woman in Italy and in France and England had been from an earlier period. After the period of the Minnesingers had passed, and the relics of knighthood had been destroyed or crumbled to dust of themselves, it was long ere anything analogous to the *donna* of Italy or the *bel esprit* of France could be found in the literature and the intercourse of people who owned the German tongue; especially in those middle-classes who gave it its great composers, or whose festivities unconsciously shaped a form of popular music in accordance with their manners. The youth's habit of wandering apprenticeship, unaccompanied, it may be remarked, by much taste for manly exercise, was followed up in married life by the man's habit of enjoying his pleasures away from home. While the willing wife remained beside the stove within the small wholesome circle of household cares, and in the less wholesome atmosphere of intercourse with her gossips, the men clubbed together in a Salique fashion, to sit, to drink, to sing. Hence the form of the male part-song. It would be superfluous here to recall how women have later struggled for their rights in Germany, with an issue for good or for evil insomuch as duty or feeling has got the upper hand—or to speak of those magnificent occasional amateur meetings in which the two halves of creation unite to honour music in its grandest vocal forms, which have flourished since a more equal distribution of the lot has been admitted.

I am merely outlining the causes which have given certain forms to what may be called National Music. These influences manifest themselves more largely in the North than in the South of the land where music was written to German words. Vienna was one-third Bohemian, one-third Hungarian, one-third Styrian, with a people more credulous, not less richly endowed with imagination of its sensual sort, but less thoughtful. Suabia and the Rhine-land possessed traditions of their own of Minnesingers and minstrels, which disposed them to a certain tuneable grace of their own, without yielding anything very peculiar in quality. The indigenous tunes of these charming districts are lively and good-humoured; the words have a dash of romance in them, but they are slight; shall I say, somewhat sickly as compared with the airs of sterner districts.

If the above affords anything like an outline of the state of society throughout Germany, it may be divined why the distinctive art-music of the land should be cultivated among the masses, and those representing our middle class, rather than be genially encouraged by the grandees; and why among native poets its highest manifestations should rather be found among the wordless inspirations of instrumental combination, than among vocal compositions.

Truth to say, the German secular part-songs for men—whether they be trade songs or student songs—are generally poor and inexpressive as compositions; owing their effect to the excellent discipline of the singers, and the heartiness with which they are sung—the joviality of the words here and there veined by some deeper meaning. They are irresistible, when first heard, by reason of their novelty : if heard at home, made all the more irresistible by the boundless hospitality of the singers. Those who surrender themselves to the humours of the countries through which they pass, without criticising habits which do not happen to be their own, will derive impressions cordial, bright, and in no common degree pleasurable, from music of the class in question, heard in its own world, and judged under its own conditions: this let me gratefully say. When considered apart from such association, the staleness, the common-place of the music, its dilutions of the national tunes, which, as I have said, possess no more striking characteristics than liveliness and geniality, forbid our assigning to it any artistic value. Here, however, is one of the freshest examples of the class.

THE RHEIN-WEIN LIED.

Andante, quasi Allegretto. RIES' *arrangement.*

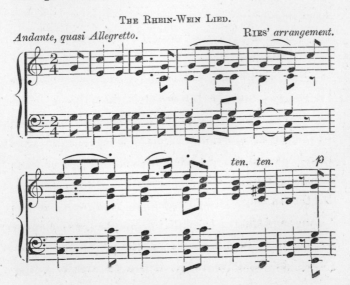

But though the materials for national music in Germany figure so incompletely in a sketch like mine, it behoves me to instance those by whom the wild spirit of old tunes has been comprehended, not merely as animating them with a force unseen, but as affording them direct types for their compositions. Beethoven could be as wondrously Hungarian in his ' Dance and Chorus ' from King Stephen, as he could be Russian in his *finale* to the A major symphony, or Eastern in his dance of the Whirling

Dervishes. Schubert, again, if I mistake not, got much inspiration from the world of the woods and of the hills. Not only do his own *lieder* bespeak this, but also (which is noticeable in reference to my argument), his predilection for Sir Walter Scott's lyrics. All know his 'Ave Maria' from 'The Lady of the Lake': his 'Coronach' from the same Scotch romance, less familiar, is no less characteristic as a wail for the dead in music. German as these songs are, there is something English in his 'Hark, the Lark' from 'Cymbeline,' something North British in his setting of those mournful lines:

> He is gone to the mountain,
>   He is lost to the forest,
> Like a summer-dried fountain,
>   When our need was the sorest.

When speaking of the National Music of Germany and its influence, it would be impossible to pass over the name of Weber, whom, I conceive, with reference to my peculiar subject, to be the most national composer of Germany.

Weber was essentially a wild composer: a man who, with all his genius and technical power as a pianist, was still imperfectly versed in the rules of his art and in the precepts of its science. He was fanciful and fantastic, as no composer before or since

himself has been ; and, by his use of the simplest
material, disguised in some degree his want of
constructive power, and the shortness of his breath,
when a melody was to be made. He had been
imperfectly taught ; he had lived an unsettled life ;
a life of vicissitude and adventure. Born in Holstein,
inefficiently trained, so far as the art and science
of music go, he had fancied more than once that he
could make out his career *without reference to music.*
He had addicted himself in his early time to the
practice and improvement of lithography, which in
those days was a new discovery ; and this failing to
satisfy his ambition, he fell back on his first inspiration, that of music, with an instinct which did
not deceive its owner.

He was a skilled and brilliant pianoforte player
who knew his instrument, though compelled to show
his knowledge thereof—let this not be forgotten—as
a court servant, while the Court of Saxony was at
dinner. He had a singular ability in inviting
attention by writing overtures of a promise as
regards the play, to which it is impossible to avoid
surrendering one's self. There are no such six
specimens so entirely different in character by
the same hand, as those by him to 'Der Frei-

schütz,' 'Preciosa,' 'Euryanthe,' 'Oberon,' the 'Jubilee Overture,' and that to 'The Ruler of the Spirits:' the last I think incomparable for the fire with which it moves, for the majesty with which it closes. There is another overture by Weber with which I am unacquainted: I mean the one to Schiller's arrangement of Carlo Gozzi's extravagant fancy-piece, 'Turandot.' The subject of this is Chinese, and it is here merely adverted to as an illustration of the preferences of its writer for that which was sharp, peculiar in its colour,—preferences which entitle him to be considered as first among what may be called national composers, or those who have produced characteristic music associated with many far distant periods, characters, and countries.

But Weber demands a separate and supreme place among the national composers of Germany, not because he gave out the scene in the 'Wolf's glen' and the Hunters' Chorus, and the demoniac glee of *Caspar*—music which drove Europe wild when it broke out, and to which it may be said the world owes an intolerable list of second-hand goblin and fairy operas, devoid alike of either terror or enchantment—but from the part-songs produced by

him in association with the soldier-poet of ' Lyre and
Sword,' Theodor Körner.

I have no need to dwell on the heroic story of this
noble young man. I have no need to recall how,
for the service of what he deemed to be the
great and good cause of his country, he broke
away from the pleasure and promise of a literary
career which was opening for him with every
prospect of success and glory, and embraced the life
of a soldier—nor how, before he fell in battle, he had
reconciled, so to say, his old with his new calling,
by producing that spirited set of songs which will
last as long as German poetry shall last.

By a happy accident, Körner's lyrics found a kindred spirit in Weber. In those set by him, the union
of words and music amounts to inspiration. The best
of the kind I know belonging to other countries—
not forgetting the ' Marseillaise,' not forgetting our
own military songs, to which I may hereafter advert,
not forgetting the feeble yet flaring Garibaldi hymn,
once so terrible to Austrian ears—are comparatively
false, characterless, and spiritless, when matched
with these.

There is the blood of a true heart in them, the
fire of a righteous courage, the song of poetry in the

prime of its vigour. The melodies are bold, new, and warlike, of a peculiarity which I find in those of no other German part-songs; and I conceive it impossible for any one to be ever so inured to excitement, ever so remote from those sympathies which breathe and burn throughout partisan nationality, to listen to these without such emotion as perhaps can be awakened neither by nature alone nor by art alone, but by the intimate union of the two, formed accidentally in some momentous juncture, thenceforth perfect and indissoluble.

MUSIC FROM THE WEST.

IF I have less novelty to offer in this my last essay, than in any former one, an obvious reason may be given. We are *at home*. I shall be of necessity also more fragmentary than heretofore, because I cannot conceive that the connection of link with link, of cause with effect, as regards manners, art, society, can require so much explanation here, as in the case of other lands. And yet there may be things in our own streets and at our own doors, as well as in our outlying districts, which are for these very reasons of familiarity overlooked.

And possibly these things may be discussed without my becoming polemical. It is to be noted, however, as a characteristic, that when we touch upon this country of ours—to wit, Great Britain, including the Principality, North Britain, and Ireland—we enter a region of anything rather than brotherly love or concord, as regards music; a region of hot controversy over our rich treasures of national melody; treasures more vast and peculiar, considering the area within which they are found, than distinguish any of the districts glanced at in my former sketches.

The amount of research brought to bear on the matter during late years is remarkable. I am not aware that the same pains has been taken with the national music of any other country. I may mention the collections of Mr. Bunting for Ireland, of Mr. Jones for Wales, certain Edinburgh publications, that of the contested Skene manuscript among the number, and the elaborate and earnest work of Mr. William Chappell on English music—an instance of twenty years' labour employed to remodel and enrich a former treatise, most honourable to the industry and enthusiasm of its writer—as works offering stores of anecdote, of special pleading, of challenges for comparison, which tend to perplex the inquirer by their number and their contradictory evidence. But I go back to my starting point: in all these cases there is something besides and beyond testimony, whether it be the testimony of manuscript or the assertion of tradition. What I remarked on the ' Marseillaise ' may be applicable in this case also.

There are family-likenesses, peculiarities of race and of physiognomy, which appeal to us with a force such as no circumstantial fending or proving can overthrow.

In my first essay I spoke of the untruthfulness of Memory. I might now call attention to the insidious pertinence of her suggestions, most especially in this matter of music. In districts lying so closely near one to the other as ours, it would not be easy to separate what may have been brought by pedlar, by stroller, by noble's retainer, from what has grown out of the soil, save on some principle of resemblance derived from observation and comparison.

In our home-world of national music I must give the first place to tunes the best known—the tunes of Wales. I find in them a remarkable grandeur and pathos, and combined with these a regularity of structure and of intervals, which set them apart from every other group of national melodies with which I am acquainted. It seems to me that no tunes have been so little tinctured by strange influences.

The solitary condition which the Welsh have preferred—their high pride of ancestry—their resolution to protract the existence of a separate language

—their defensive habits in point of litigation—the somewhat remote beauty of their district, which has features and attractions of its own—these things have all conspired to retain in the music of the Principality a certain primitive character. I think that while Irishmen and Scotchmen have been fighting for certain airs, and while, of late, Englishmen have been rushing in to get as much credit for England out of Ireland and Scotland as there was any chance of getting, no one has laid hands on the tunes of Wales; no one has said, in regard to any particular melody, 'This is a tune which may have got into *your* country, but which is *our* tune.'

The symmetry of the Welsh tunes distinguishes them from those of Scotland and Ireland. In the latter there is a perversity of interval and of modulation, which may be partly ascribed to imperfect transcription, but not altogether. In the Welsh tunes I cannot recall a single irregular sequence, or a single rhythm awry. In many of them there is to be remarked the old mechanical progression, 'Alla Rosalia,' which it seems especially the province of the harp to encourage; in others, as in 'The Rising of the Lark,' there are phrases of six against eight bars; but withal, and bearing as they do an unmistakable family likeness one to the other, they have a certain stately evenness, without insipidity, which gives great pleasure.

The instrument of Wales, the harp, has lent itself largely to this symmetrical formation, because it is not an incomplete instrument. With its three rows of strings—the third, so far as I understand, anticipating the pedals of the modern harp, by which accidental flats and sharps are now procured—there is little temptation for those caprices of interval which have been generated by instruments with a drone, such as the bagpipe, or by stringed ones less elaborate in facture.

The charm of the harp is not merely such as belongs to the intimate correspondence betwixt master and servant which it seems to encourage, but in its own peculiar tones. It has, I think, been too much undervalued in our day, because of its limited powers in modulation. The harp, however, continues to be one of the primitive sources of melody, not merely because of its peculiar tone, but because of its simplicity of scale. The following is not one of the more rare tunes, but not therefore the less beautiful.

But if the harp tunes of Wales are what may be called players' tunes—melodies, that is, referable to the cultivation of a peculiar instrument, with a scale and a behaviour and conditions of its own—the Principality has its singers' tunes likewise, and those of great vocal purity and clearness.

Here is a thoroughly attractive melody, which does not bear a trace of age or singularity:—

A remarkable collection was made some years ago, by an accomplished lady belonging to the Neath Valley—Miss Maria Jane Williams, of Aberpergwm, whom I may further mention as having been one of the most exquisite amateur singers of any country, aware of her own powers—within her own world, perfect. Being a thorough musician, and as tenaciously imbued with home love as a woman, and a Welshwoman, can be, her notation of the tunes which were published by her, I think, may be relied on.

One of these melodies, 'The Blackbird,' reputed to be of great age, will remind the hearer of some half-dozen well-known tunes: of the English one, 'Pretty Polly Oliver,' with its namby-pamby verses, 'Fair Hebe I left with a cautious design;' of the Irish 'Last Rose of Summer,' distilled by Moore out of 'The Groves of Blarney.'

I have purposely chosen this specimen, which has hitherto not found its way into collections, as one of the many examples of coincidence and comparison which entirely baffle the dogmatist who pretends to decide on national melody. There are certainly few other Welsh tunes which bear resemblance to 'The Blackbird.' It is remarkable for its three-bar phrases:—

It may be observed that, though the Welsh will dance twelve hours at a Christmas frolic to the tune of 'Sweet Richard' (I speak from experience and without exaggeration), the country has no dance of its own; such as the 'Irish Jig' (performed on the door taken from its hinges), such as the Scotch Reel, such as the English Hornpipe.

That a great composer could turn Welsh tunes
to good account, is proved in Handel's *English* 'Acis
and Galatea' (there was also an Italian version of
the story by him), and in his 'Deborah.' The
choruses 'Happy we' and 'O Baal' are clearly
referable to the tune called in Wales 'The Rising
Sun,' in which, as in the other tune, 'Of a noble
race was Shenkin,' the naked figure of bass accompaniment, or call it a ground bass, stands out.

With this melody Handel may have made
acquaintance, owing to his intimacy with the Gran-
ville family. But it is remarkable that so few have
got beyond the boundaries of this country, as 'Auld
lang syne' and 'The Last Rose of Summer' have
done from Scotland and Ireland. And yet Mr.
Thomson of Edinburgh, a man who seems to have
been far in advance of his time, committed a large collection of the best known airs to Haydn for arrangement, and the same were published with words by
song-writers no less eminent than Burns, Campbell,
Scott, Joanna Baillie, Professor Smyth of Cambridge,
Mrs. John Hunter, Mrs. Opie, Mrs. Grant. From
the masterly neatness with which the writer of the
'Canzonets' handled these old melodies, it may be
inferred that he was fully aware of their musical

adaptability; yet still they are unknown abroad. No Boieldieu, or Niedermeyer, or Flotow has thought it worth while to eke out his own tenuity of invention, or to give a morsel of local colour, by consulting so remarkable a treasury of national melodies.

There is a modern French opera, ' Nabab,' the same which assisted to bring forward the exquisitely finished accomplishments of Madame Miolan Carvalho, the scene of which is partly laid in Wales. Here, what is called ' the local colour' resolved itself into a snuff manufactory, with a vine above the door, and a young lady in a *tartan* scarf, who sung as a *bravura* in praise of tobacco, no sweet Welsh melody, but a sharply-cut Parisian tune. I do not remember a single Welsh air on the English stage during the last five and twenty years, save the one introduced by Mr. Charles Mathews into one of the Olympic dramas.

One cause of such oversight may be found in the persevering (why not say, obstinate?) insulation within which our neighbour-subjects, by way of asserting pedigree, have coffered up, and clamped and chained their nationality. Surely, in these days, when intercourse must be rapid, when the world can be for no one's pleasure or pride

parcelled out into separate parishes, each of which
is resolute to take the law of the others, the proceedings of Welsh patrons of art are subject to
the inquiry—how far it is self-importantly made a toy?
—how far they are willing to fall into the great stream
of time which *will* bear onward ourselves, our pomps
and vanities, and our works—good only as they in-
struct and fertilise those who are to come after us?

Gower, Chaucer's predecessor, a Welshman, our
first poet, wrote in *English*. If his countrymen do
not discard him as an apostate, is there not here
pedigree, precedent, example to every real lover of
national Welsh art?

And now, to cross the Channel: and on arriving
in the world of Irish music, we find ourselves in a
wild world in every sense of the word. The antiquaries, the claimants—authorities who profess to
understand Phœnician, or to date their ancestry from
Spain, so beset the inquirer after nationality, that
he has to keep a calm head, and a keen pair of eyes
in the same, if he looks into the matter.

A wild world, I repeat, but one as lovely as wild;
full of every gracious natural product—a world
which knew the fairy charms of harp and pipe and
symphony from an early period—a world full of

tune, full of genius, full of capacity; less full, we critical English may say, of the cementing common sense which brings all these charming elements together in music.

I cannot pretend to form a guess whether the practice and proficiency of the harp, one of the two oldest instruments, dates back to an elder period in Ireland or in Wales. Mr. Bunting, who gathered many facts concerning it from the real old harpers surviving at the close of the last century, assures us that so early as the fourteenth century the instrument had thirty strings, in compass ranging betwixt C and D in *alt.* This is the date given to the richly ornamented instrument preserved in Trinity College, Dublin, played on by O'Neill through the streets of Limerick in 1760. Mr. Bunting names five different species of harps—the common harp, the high-headed harp, the down-bending harp, a portable harp used in ecclesiastical ceremonies, and the harp of Craftin. (I think this may have been Crofton, renowned in Irish legends.) This Irish harp had its imperfections and inconsistencies; no string for F sharp between E and G in the bass; only two of the major keys perfect in their diatonic intervals. It was tuned, too, in an odd old traditional way. Here is what would

be called in these days a study or a prelude, called
'Try if it is in tune.'

Quick and Spirited.

This at once suggests the seeming caprice, the real deficiency of certain intervals, which mark a large section of the tunes of Ireland, probably the most ancient ones; such as the following, which professes to be a 'Lamentation.' The large share, by the way, which popular, not Church, music has taken and takes in mourning for the dead in Ireland, is a characteristic not to be overlooked.

This form of tunes then grew out of instrumental inequality. How curiously contrasted with the tunes of the East, which are only regular *when* instrumental! On the other hand, a vocabulary, an ordinance of these, must have existed in the country from a very remote period. The Irish, as well as the Welsh, have a dictionary of musical terms of their own. In this will be found such entries as these: 'Lulling Music,' 'Music of cool shade,' 'Wilderness,' 'Watery Plain,' 'Lake Music,' 'Musical Fear,' 'Flowing tide strain,' 'High wailing strain,' (Lamentation again). There are half a hundred definitions as picturesque and fantastic as the above. There is little or nothing equivalent that I know of in any other language, save perhaps the phrases which regulate the proceedings of those who contrive such mysterious matters as the music and the doings of our Christmas pantomimes, because among these occur such directions as ‘Hurry,’ ‘Lively Trips,’ and others.

If something such as has been described was the ancient harp—if such may have been the traditions by which it was ruled—what were the harpers? A great number of them were blind men : the harp has always been an instrument dear to the blind, because there is an intimacy in its strings to the player, and it is one among the thousand admirable compensations in this unequal world of ours, that the blind seem to be born musicians. And many of these Irish harpers, Bunting tells us, were poor relations belonging to good families, who had to make out their livelihoods in a fashion more independent than was the life of the ‘ Led Captain,’ who sat at the foot of the squire’s table to laugh at the squire’s jokes, to carve the squire’s haunch, and to live by the squire’s bounty. These Irish harpers could give an equivalent for shelter, food, and countenance. They could give a grace to the festivities of rough queer carousal by their music. They were in request everywhere, more than I conceive the more complete Welsh harpers to have been.

One crossed into Scotland, a certain Rory Dall, in regard to whose country Hibernian and Scot have fought fiercely: and about whom there is some terrible controversial tradition that he may have played the harp to the lady of many legends, Mary of Scotland; as if she had not among her foreign retainers imported an Italian harper called Rizzio. Rory Dall is said to have left his harp and its tuning key in Scotland. Echlin Kane was another of these men, a blind Irish harper that wandered over the world, got so far as France, Spain, and Italy, was patronised by the Pretender, and complimented by Lord Macdonald of Skye, by a present of Rory Dall's silver tuning key; but who was such a riotous personage when in Lord Macdonald's house (the blind are often doubly riotous *because* of the loss of their eyes), '*that the Highland Jacobite gentry found it occasionally necessary to repress his turbulence by cutting his nails, and so rendering him unable to play till they grew again to their proper length.*'

I said that the Irish had from an early period 'harp, and pipe, and symphony.' Their pipe was the bagpipe again, the same pipe as belongs to Calabria,

o

to the Basque provinces of France, and to Scotland;
a sort of ubiquitous musical creature.   But the bagpipe was the military instrument in Ireland.
Whereas the Welsh marches—*vide* the 'March of
the Men of Harlech'—are harp tunes in grand
common time, there is a sort of queer, odd, Rapparee
humour in the Irish pipe marches.   The following,
reported to be very ancient, in $\frac{6}{8}$ time, bears as a
tune a close resemblance to the impassioned jig
danced by a wild bare-legged pair, on the cabin door
taken off its hinges, of which mention is to be found
in the tales of Miss Edgeworth, Lady Morgan, and
Griffin.

Very soft.

I cannot fancy a more efficient engine of torment to one's foes than this tune.

But besides these incoherent and ranting measures, ascribable to a strange harp and to vulgar pipers, Irish music contains many delicious tunes, attractive because of their regularity, delicately tender, and rarely sweet: many of these are in old rhythms. There is the melody, 'At the mid-hour of night'—to recall Moore's words—which consists of five lines of five-bar phrases, the same containing one five-bar phrase three times repeated, another twice repeated. There is a tune called 'John, heir of the

glen;' there is 'The pretty girl milking her cow,'
—both in triple rhythm. But the following, from
Mr. Bunting's collection, has not, I think, been set
to words. At all events, it is very charming.

Certain melodies are more regular still; and
among these, one on the simple notes of the scale,
than which no tune has been more fiercely fought
for by Scot and Hibernian. I mean ' Robin Adair,'
—the tune which Catalani varied—which Boieldieu

introduced into his 'Les deux nuits'—to which Moore bent himself to write a national and patriotic melody—and which Burns fitted with some of his smoothest words :

Had I a cave on some far-distant shore.

There is no need to present it, with its extreme simplicity of intervals in a strain thrice repeated, and with the episode which breaks this. I mention it with another purpose, because, strange to say, neither Moore (who failed in 'The Exile of Erin,' after Campbell had written it), nor Burns—neither Hibernian bard nor Scottish ploughman treated the simple tune so well in song as did an English Peer, Lord Thurlow,—the Lord Thurlow over whose volume of verse Moore himself and Byron are said to have sat up at midnight, screaming with ridicule. Be the rest of his volume ever so good, ever so bad, there are few things in English better for music than the two opening verses. And since mention of words for music has been made, I cannot leave the subject of Irish melody without calling attention to the wonderful verbal productions which have been written to some of the original melodies of Ireland. All our world over, popular minstrels have somehow harboured a distracted idea that they were becoming courtly and poetical if they had to do with Hector and Andromache. Burns was not exempt from this tawdry taste : as when writing :—

> O saw ye bonnie Lesley,
> As she gaed o'er the border,
> *She's gone like Alexander,*
> To spread her conquests further.

But the Hibernian rhymesters, besides being magnificent, have been in so small degree confused; and have heaped together verbs, images, metaphors, great names of antiquity, with a hardihood such as I think has no parallel.

One of the most dismal Irish tunes in my acquaintance—one of the few really dismal Irish tunes that I know—is called the ' Dear Irish maid.' I think the tune to be nearly as dismal as our own English Christmas Carol, the burden of which is tidings of

> practical comfort and joy.

The native words, as sung at Cork, to this tune, form a long ballad, describing a walk ' At the hour of prime, when Morpheus was parting,' taken by a minstrel in a ' vernal valley,' wherein he observes the charming heroine, whose perfections, and the course of his respectful wooing, he proceeds to chronicle. I cannot resist citing a couple of verses.

The gentleman having observed the lady, afterwards
approaches her:

> I guessed her not Venus, Minerva, or Helen,
> Calypso, Eucarius,[16] or fair Eurydice.
> Her dress appeared rural, as there she sat viewing
> A meand'ring brook that most rapidly glides.
> My spirits recruiting, I approached with confusion,
> And gently saluted this seraphic fair.
> She said, ' Sir, pass by me, and don't tantalise me,
> For by love I'm destined to repine in these shades.'

He goes on, not rebuffed:

> Are you Sylvia or Pandora, sage Pallas or Flora,
> Hibernia or Scotia; or *what* is your name?
> Or are you famed Juno, or bright shining Luna,
> Or are you a human of Adam's great race?'

To whom the lady, as follows:—

> With mild condescension, and smiles on each feature,
> She said, ' Sir, *be seated in these lonely green bowers,*
> *As I am no deity,* but a plain country maiden
> That sallied forth early to gather some flowers;
> These copious plantations and bounties of Ceres
> Have so pre-engaged me at this hour of day,
> That I roved out more careless, led on by Dame Nature,
> So excuse the frailties of a dear Irish maid.'

The rhyme and the reason of this lyric (there are
three verses of it) are noteworthy, as illustrating the
characteristic national confusion which has had
much to do with national music.

The fact of a people so overflowing with fun and
humour and repartee being dead to the absurdity of
such bothered Arcadian minstrelsy as the above,

[16] *Sic.*—Ed.

strikes me with surprise as often as I advert to it. I know of nothing so flagrant in the popular ballads of England, Scotland, or Wales—nor even among the Negro melodies.

There is another singularity which I have been unable to explain; the weary want of tune and accent distinguishing Irish singers. They never seem willing to come to an end of their delights and devices. I have noted the same peculiarity as characterising the players of a heavier people, the people of Belgium. I imagine, to protract the sound and the words is conceived to be as Arcadian and genteel as the use of grand Greek classical names may have been fancied by the rhymester without rhyme who wove the wondrous piece of stuff, a shred of which I have just presented.

If I speak within a smaller compass than might be expected of the music of Scotland, I do so because it is national music better known than that of either Wales or Ireland. Even on the Continent, Scottish music is the term applied to all the national airs of this country. In a collection arranged by Beethoven will be found ' Of a noble race was Shenkin,' 'The last rose of Summer,' and absolutely, ' Sally in our alley,' thus designated by one common epithet.

This is be accounted for by the fact, that Scotland had a civilised Court of her own till a late period; and that thus the products of the North country were naturally more largely interchanged with those of other European countries, than could be the products of exclusive Wales or of careless, harassed Ireland.

Boieldieu twisted about their tunes largely in his 'La Dame Blanche,' a comical *pasticcio* from 'The Monastery,' and in 'Les deux nuits.' Niedermeyer set most pleasantly 'Auld Lang Syne' as a *villanella* in his 'Marie Stuart.' I have found as a rule, that whenever our national music is mentioned on the Continent, the tune has been approved with a complacent 'Oui, c'est Ecossais;' and two minutes after, something is sure to follow about the 'Bride of Lammermoor,' although the tunes had got abroad before the greatest novel of the Great Unknown was written.

I must name as among the most complete examples of national forms turned to musical order, the *Scherzo* of Mendelssohn's Third Symphony in A minor, called from this very *Scherzo* 'the Scottish' Symphony, as his Second Symphony was called Italian because of its final *Saltarella*.

But then, if foreigners have laid a wholesale claim on all *our* tunes as Scotch tunes, they have also chosen to ascribe to some of the best of North British melodies a foreign origin.

Rizzio, say they, brought over his Italian science and skill into Mary Stuart's Court, and from this issued modes and habits that altered the cast of the Northern melodies. A more baseless fancy, I conceive, never entered mortal brain. Let us look at a fact or two :

Rizzio was a harper. There is small trace of the harp in the old Scottish melodies, which are wild, wandering, containing all manner of illogical intervals and incomplete closes ; thus serving, so far as I can guess (recalling former definitions), to be a sort of compound of the chant set to words of fresh and real beauty, with the sounds of a rude instrument— the pipe.

And though, as has been said, the presence of Irish harpers may have been occasional, if not frequent, in Scotland, I do not find many traces of the harp-spirit in the tunes of Scotland, beyond that similarity in the omission of certain intervals which has reference to one common origin, and which may have caused many of the fierce national contests, undertaken with the vague hope of settling the birthplace of melodies which probably belong to neither one country or the other, but to both.

But I think that the Scotch may be said to have trained up the bagpipe to a perfection of superiority, and to keep up that perfection even unto this day. And I conceive that one of those grand, stalwart practitioners whom we see in that magnificent costume which English folks have not disdained to wear (though it is a relic belonging to a peculiar district), would blow down, by the force and persistence of his drone, any rival from Calabria, or the Basque Provinces, or the centre of France, or the Sister Island.

To this universal bagpipe may some of the lawless progressions of Scottish melodies be referred. The following is clearly a relation to the Irish march on three legs already cited.

Let me now speak of a peculiarity in Scottish music, which I doubt not has suggested itself to the reader before I have named it: *the snap*, or rapid succession of two notes :—

and so forth.

With regard to the origin of this, I have always nourished a fancy born of my own experience.

There are singers who when they attempt to recollect a melody *try to reproduce a harmony also*— to present to themselves *a duet*; and this can only be done by catching at either the principal or accessory note (as may be), before or after the sound has been emitted.

I have never been able to represent to my solitary self the tune of a two-part song without some such ease to imagination, if not to conscience; and thus, as the figure rarely occurs with any use of an awkward interval, I dare to conceive that it may have originated with a player's habit, as among players who *spread* all their chords, or with a singer's trick.

This figure is predominant in Scottish airs of a certain class, but it is not exclusively Scottish. One can find it in Italy, though perhaps not before Rizzio's or Ricci's time. And see how oddly definitions and coincidences turn up! The form occurs in a sort of sacred song by Pergolesi, called *Siciliana* :—

I presume that in the above, the figure may have been meant to stand for a sob. In any event, the figure is rarely to be met in conjunction with a false concord. Nor is it frequent in Italian, howbeit perpetual in Scotch music.

Some of the least-contested Scotch tunes are remarkable in the extent of their compass. I wil merely remind the reader of such melodies as ' For the lack of gold,' ' Whistle o'er the lave o't.'

The Scotch dances, whether the frantic reel or stately strathspey, are mostly in *common time*; and, indeed, the triple measure figures sparingly in their music as compared with the music of Ireland. It

has some capital examples though, as in 'Tweed-
side,' with those amazing words :—

> What beauty does Flora disclose,
>> How sweet are her smiles upon Tweed,
> But Mary's, yet sweeter than those,
>> Both Nature and Fancy exceed.

In the above there is the three-bar rhythm. I
only recollect one other example, in the song
'Wooed and married and a'.'

As regards tenderness of expression and grace of
interval, the Irish and the Scotch may keep up the
old tough fight as to which is the tenderest. But
the tune I shall now present is surely as gracious,
and quite with a colour of its own, as the Irish
specimen which I cited :—

Lastly, there are certain Scottish tunes reputed
to be Cameronian, which I dare say may have been
fabricated long after the civil strife of creeds, so
wondrously set forth in 'Old Mortality,' had ceased,
but which are still neither English, Irish, nor Welsh.
The tune which I offer has in some measure the
character and the sadness, without the austerity, of
such a Psalm as was sung at Loudon Hills :—

I cannot but feel as if I were faithless to the reel as a dance measure, in passing it over as I must do in a subject full of what some old author calls 'pastime and particularity'; but I am unable to do more than to touch a point here and there.

On looking over Mr. Chappell's collection of English tunes, I have been struck anew, as I have been again and again in former years, by the want of a style which establishes a certain parentage, as that by which French, Italian, and Northern melodies are affiliated, or by which the Scotch and Irish, or Welsh airs are recognisable.

I say this with all respect to the sincerity of the writer, but, with reference to a partisanship which is natural in one who has fixed his eyes on a single point. *He* conceives record in print to decide the parentage of a tune. I do not. The 'Pastoral Symphony' in the 'Messiah' was printed in 'Parthenia,' as a dance, long ere Handel dreamed of appropriating the tune of the Roman or Calabrian *pifferari* for his 'Nativity' scene. Who prompted the printer? is the question. And it is a question which no one can answer, so far as national music is concerned.

Now, so far as Mr. Chappell's diligently prepared

and most agreeably written book represents English music, it is therein represented as eminently eclectic.

I think we get from it the measure of 'Sir Roger de Coverley,' and a hornpipe tune—with that shuffle on the floor which is not *dancing* so much as getting over the ground; but I find among the English tunes nothing in the least equivalent to Welsh or Irish or Scotch melodies, as regards freshness or strangeness, or the character which distinguishes the little woman in the red cloak and hat from the Highlander in his kilt.

Let us see, if we can, if there be originating causes for this. A nation of shopkeepers, as we have been contemptuously called, we are still a nation of travellers, gentle and simple; and travellers who, while curious as to things abroad, are wondrously constant to our home notions. With all our good faith, there may be some pertinacity in us; some inaptitude to digest impressions alien to those of nature and education.

The author of 'Tremaine' called us 'slow to move,' and this long after one Shakspeare had put into the mouth of a certain *Portia* a character in which there was more of Shakspeare's own intuition than the perception of the Italian heiress of Belmont, brilliant as she was. Speaking of the Englishman, says Shakspeare's Portia : 'I say nothing to *him*, for he understands not *me* nor I him. He hath neither *Latin, French,* nor *Italian.* I think he bought his doublet in *Italy,* his round hose in *France,* his bonnet in *Germany,* and his behaviour everywhere.'

There are many English tunes which may belong to nobody or to everybody.

If the speculations which I have presented have any thread (so to say) on which, as so many entire and separate yet not disparted beads they can be strung, it is this : that nationality in music does not lie in either borrowing or in adaptation, but in some inborn qualities to be ascribed either to the influences of Nature or of manners, or of peculiar instruments, originated by rude people. There is small trace of anything of the kind in English music. I belong to the North, and know the good and sweet quality of our Lancashire voices, but where is the Lancashire tune? and where is the Cumberland tune?

As illustrating the caprice of Music's proceeding in all countries, it is observable that in England our art got ahead of Painting ; since the Elizabethan madrigals, in which there are many national touches, came long before the establishment of a kindred

school of art; our school of Painting dating only
from the last century.   Whereas in Italy the painters
had long preceded the musicians, in England the
musicians had enjoyed their primrose-time, if not
their June or their Indian summer, long ere the
painter was known except by the stiff outline on the
wall, howsoever well intentioned, meagre in form
and paltry in colour. Our travelled men, such as
Milton, had brought home fancies. Our abiding
patrons, such as Lord Guildford, George Herbert,
the high-toned Evelyn, the convenient, gossiping,
yet altogether delightful Pepys, opened their minds
to this player on the lute, or the other foreign
song, or vocal enchantments of 'the Italian gentle-
woman who would not be kissed, which Master
Killigrew, who brought her in, did acquaint us with;'
long ere painting had got beyond the stiffest of
stiff Gothicism.   And again : that beautiful and
harmonious architect—I mean Wren—to whom we
owe the exquisitely harmonious outer cupola of
St. Paul's, and St. Stephen's, Walbrook, and a host
of other eclectic examples, could arise and vindicate
himself, and produce (to hunt the figure a few steps
further) a host of *melodious* details in stone, after the
Revolution, with its Ironsides and its fanatics, had

purged out of the land the lute in the oriel window, the pleasant part-song in the pleachèd walk, or even those astounding lessons by Dr. John Bull, tabulated in Queen Elizabeth's 'Virginal Book,' which I take leave to believe Queen Elizabeth may have looked at, but can never have played.

From the time of the Restoration Music began again to raise her head in England, though checked again by the sarcasms of what has been so strangely called our 'Augustan age;' but never, whether her head was high or low, has melody worn in this land of ours that distinct family face of her own which is to be found in Wales, Ireland, or Scotland. That which we have enjoyed seems to me referable to every country or district save those of pure England—with some exception.

And, following out this idea, I am afraid that I shall shock some of my readers by saying that all the old snatches of song in Shakspeare's plays seem more questionable than characteristic. Mr. Chappell himself points out that *Ophelia's* snatch of song, 'And *he* will not come again,' is identical with a tune the burden of which is, 'And *she* cannot hold her tongue.' I can add, it closely resembles a third melody, 'Sweet Nelly, my heart's delight.'

I must go an heretical step further, as we are on
the subject of Shakspeare music, and confess cool
disrespect in regard to the far-famed music for
'Macbeth,' said to be Locke's—more probably by
Eccles: in no event of parentage worth quarrelling
about.   But, for exceptions, I must name Dr. Arne's
music to 'The Tempest,' and to 'As you like it:'
'Where the bee sucks,' and 'Blow, blow, thou winter
wind,' are English words set to English music, with
as much freshness and originality as beauty.

Then, as I have by chance diverged into this
path, I must represent that Bishop's settings of
Shakspeare are by themselves in power and in
freshness.   His 'Bid me discourse' is the most
lasting English bravura in being; his delicious
canzonet, 'By the simplicity of Venus' doves,' (a
most exquisite setting of sound to sense) and
his 'Orpheus' duet owe little save to English
inspiration.

Bishop had a fairy land of his own.   Peculiarities
of character only stood between him and a European
fame.   And then he fell on evil days, when the riches
of the continent were streaming into England; and
when those in whose service his life was passed,
tempted, and perhaps constrained him to make

concessions to our then poor popular taste : a luck-less and foolish thing, if it be done by any artist in defiance of conscience ; a sad thing, if it be done with *acquiescence of conscience.*

The very great and English beauty of Bishop's music—always the best when his words were the best—makes me recall his career with sadness, as though it was an imperfect career.

Among our peculiar treasures is the glee, as distinguished from the madrigal ; the part-song for the voices of the human quartett. That this form has been abused by a puerile mode of treatment, has nothing to do with its intrinsic beauty. I am not going to travel through the 'Convito Armonico,' but I will just remind the reader of Stevens' exquisite setting of 'Ye spotted snakes,' and mention the most perfect example of a glee-writer that England *has* possessed—since of those who are happily still living I should conceive it unbecoming to speak. I allude to Horsley : an artist who passed away from us full of years, only lately ; and who was laid in his grave in the midst of respectful friends, retained throughout a patriarch's life by an uprightness which was not to be shaken, and by musical endowments of pure quality and high order.

I revert to him for many reasons. He had the true poetical appreciation now in an ailing plight among our composers, who do not seem to heed whether they waste a melody on the pence-table or a scrap of advertisement from the ' Times.'

Horsley set few, if any, save choice words, *but these he set most choicely* : writing beautifully. as regards science, with a true national relish, which neither cared to be German, nor knew how to be French, nor disdained the sweetness of Italy—that fountain of great vocal writing. I will name his glees, ' See the chariot,' ' Nymphs of the forest,' ' By Celia's arbour,' as so many gems, showing a modest constructive persistence not too common among our glee writers, who, to give as an instance ' When winds breathe soft,' have seemed to fancy that every second line must have another movement. And I will name his canons, as having an ease, an elegance, and a mastery, which entitle them to be placed not far from the vocal canons of Cherubini, and the instrumental concealments of art by art which are so remarkable in the canons of Clementi.

There is yet another form of English music which I think no Scotch moss-trooper can inter-meddle with—no Irish reaper can deprive us of—no

Welsh antiquary carry away into the fastnesses of the Principality : the catch. The odd farcical humour of this form of musical composition, in which words trip up words, and rhymes and phrases jostle, with as desperate a disregard of common sense as though Hood had wrought the web and sown it thick with puns—can hardly be appreciated by any one save he be an Englishman born.

It is noticeable that we have never produced a great instrumental composer, neither a *towering* player on any instrument. Plenty of hand work there has been, plenty of industry ; but till now there has been too universal an exhibition of hands without head, or else of head without hands. Why this should be, others must decide.

As a people who can read at sight, we are without superiors or equals. Our voices are beautiful, and I think almost more equally distributed as respects the register than the voices of any other country. I will instance those of Mrs. Salmon, Mrs. Alfred Shaw, Braham, Bartleman—not, for obvious reasons, to speak of any singers still giving pleasure to the public—as almost unparagoned, and as in every case cultivated to a certain point of versatile accomplishment. I have had to point out, however, on a former occasion, how largely this has been neutralised, and has not passed a certain point, owing to a want of clearness and refinement in articulation.

And lastly, as dealing with this portion of my subject, I must speak of our English patrons of music. We have had—we have to this day—munificent upholders of the art, great amateurs. I need not recall such a man as the patron of Handel, the Marquis of Chandos; who did that utterly heterodox deed of creating a Protestant Chapel-music at his own cost, with evil fiddles in the orchestra; by whom Handel was cherished and promoted, and for whom he wrote his noble anthems. I need not mention such a series of London gentlemen as scrambled up to the garret of Thomas Britton, the small-coal man, to hear chamber-music. I need not mention such a stocking weaver of Leicester as Mr. Gardiner, who was certainly, next to Burney, among the first men in England to discern the remarkable force and fire of Beethoven as a composer; and who innocently proposed to the rude hermit of Vienna that he should prefix to a sort of compilation from Beethoven's works, made by the said Mr. Gardiner, an original overture; to be well paid for. These facts speak for England's taste, honour, knowledge, and *prescience as it was* in the days when the practice of the art here was limited.

Now, when the love and culture of music are grown again to be something like a household word, it is singular to mark how the prescience has become timid, how curiosity has been dulled, how research has stopped. *Being virtuous, ' there are to be no more cakes and ale.'* And so, at the time being—with all the vast mechanical resources of this country, and with its prodigious wealth waiting for the lap of any man, woman, or child who will hold the apron open —it is singular to see combined an exclusiveness which in past poorer times did not exist. We have a vast public now, for four or five composers: Handel, Mozart, Beethoven, Mendelssohn, and Signor Rossini (in his elect works). We may admire too deeply as *partisans*: we may be too unwilling to admire three things instead of two; and therefore, with all our honesty, our wealth, our welcome—and *now*, our great and widely diffused musical culture— we may fail for a while—not for the future, I earnestly believe—betwixt eclecticism and exclusiveness, in having a music of our own.

It was my intention to attempt some outline of the forms of music in America; but on looking closer

I find therein such a heap of disconnected elements —French, German, English-Puritan, and Negro; music of times old and times new, without any present individuality, that I will forbear to enter into a maze of which no living person seems as yet to hold the clue.

Such character as the people of the country have shown in their imaginative literature seems not as yet to have wrought itself out in art, or only capriciously. Their Painting has as yet no Washington Irving—their Music is till now without its Nathaniel Hawthorne. Though they are full of instincts for singing, both the white and the dark population—as was shown to us most quaintly by the Hutchinson family, and later to satiety by the parties who have called up a host of imitators, and have degraded the sentimental word 'Serenader' into something suggestive of a *monkey and a blacking brush*—there is as yet surprisingly little either in their song-words or music that can be called their own. I believe that I possess the largest collection of 'Little Warblers' from across the Atlantic, that could be found in England; and with the exception of a slang song or two, such as I can fancy made by a machine in our parish of St. Giles', I find nothing newer or more fresh in words or melody than 'Woodman, spare that tree.'

The Americans have shown a marvellous proclivity, in instrumental music, towards that which is occult and incomprehensible; and, to judge from what reaches the old country in the shape of printed opinion, are already far in advance of us in comprehending that which seems full of darkness and doubt to our eyes. Whether in this they are not beginning at the end of music, may be reserved for others to decide.

As a close to these essays, which are only within their permitted dimensions so many mere sketches, I may be allowed to point attention to the subject as one the richness of which renders it almost intractable.

To prepare them, I have looked through between two and three thousand tunes, and thus can feel better than most of my readers *how* much could have been said; *how* much I have of necessity been obliged to omit.

LONDON : PRINTED BY
SPOTTISWOODE AND CO., NEW-STREET SQUARE
AND PARLIAMENT STREET

Small post 8vo. 3s. 6d.

A

TEXT-BOOK OF HARMONY.

FOR SCHOOLS AND STUDENTS.

By C. E. HORSLEY.

REVISED BY WESTLEY RICHARDS AND W. H. CALCOTT.

SATURDAY REVIEW.

' The work seems well adapted to beginners, and puts the relations of our scale and harmony in a clear and easily apprehended form.'

MUSICAL STANDARD.

'A posthumous work of an accomplished musician. . . . May be regarded as a safe book.'

MUSICAL TIMES.

' Mr. Horsley was a highly-accomplished musician. . . . It may be regarded as the latest development of his ideas upon the theory of the art of which he was so able a professor. . . . Some of the observations, too, upon the method in which pupils should work are worthy of notice, for, apart from his own musical acquirements, it must be remembered that Mr. Horsley was intimately acquainted with Spohr, Mendelssohn, Hauptmann, &c., and we all know how much the character is moulded by constant intercourse with the aristocracy of art.'

London: SAMPSON LOW, MARSTON, SEARLE, & RIVINGTON, Crown Buildings, 188 Fleet Street, E.C.

THE

'MUSICAL CURRICULUM.'

By GEO. F. ROOT.

A 'NEW DEPARTURE' IN THE ART OF
MUSIC TEACHING.

––––––––

IT goes to work on the plan that pupils should not be
made to pursue their studies in the tedious, mechanical
methods, which, while making the fingers supple, dwarf
and warp the mental faculties. The 'MUSICAL CURRICULUM'
early opens up the beauties of the theory of music, and
gives the pupil glimpses of the science, while it teaches the
art. The gradual development of the subject is fascinating;
at every step something is gained, and that something is
clearly defined and exemplified. Whatever is of an abstract
nature is continually relieved by the introduction of pleasing
exercises or *songs*, which, while constantly progressing,
furnish also agreeable relaxation.

8vo. cloth extra, 15s.

––––––––

London : SAMPSON LOW, MARSTON, SEARLE, & RIVINGTON,
Crown Buildings, 188 Fleet Street, E.C.

𝔄 𝔏𝔦𝔰𝔱 𝔬𝔣 𝔅𝔬𝔬𝔨𝔰

PUBLISHED BY

SAMPSON LOW, MARSTON, SEARLE, & RIVINGTON.

ALPHABETICAL LIST.

A CLASSIFIED Educational Catalogue of Works published in Great Britain. Demy 8vo, cloth extra. Second Edition, revised and corrected to Christmas, 1878, 5*s.*

Abney (Captain W. de W., R.E., F.R.S.) Thebes, and its Five Greater Temples. Forty large Permanent Photographs, with descriptive letter-press. Super-royal 4to, cloth extra, 63*s.*

About Some Fellows. By an ETON BOY, Author of "A Day of my Life." Cloth limp, square 16mo, 2*s.* 6*d.*

Adventures of Captain Mago. A Phœnician's Explorations 1000 years B.C. By LEON CAHUN. Numerous Illustrations. Crown 8vo, cloth extra, gilt, 7*s.* 6*d.*

Adventures of a Young Naturalist. By LUCIEN BIART, with 117 beautiful Illustrations on Wood. Edited and adapted by PARKER GILLMORE. Post 8vo, cloth extra, gilt edges, New Edition, 7*s.* 6*d.*

Afghanistan and the Afghans. Being a Brief Review of the History of the Country, and Account of its People. By H. W. BELLEW, C.S.I. Crown 8vo, cloth extra, 6*s.*

Alcott (Louisa M.) Jimmy's Cruise in the "Pinafore." With 9 Illustrations. Small post 8vo, cloth gilt, 3*s.* 6*d.*

—— *Aunt Jo's Scrap-Bag.* Square 16mo, 2*s.* 6*d* (Rose Library, 1*s.*)

—— *Cupid and Chow-Chow.* Small post 8vo, 3*s.* 6*d.*

—— *Little Men: Life at Plumfield with Jo's Boys.* Small post 8vo, cloth, gilt edges, 3*s.* 6*d.* (Rose Library, Double vol. 2*s.*)

—— *Little Women.* 1 vol., cloth, gilt edges, 3*s.* 6*d.* (Rose Library, 2 vols., 1*s.* each.)

—— *Old-Fashioned Girl.* Best Edition, small post 8vo, cloth extra, gilt edges, 3*s.* 6*d.* (Rose Library, 2*s.*)

A

Alcott (Louisa M.) Work and Beginning Again. A Story of Experience. 1 vol., small post 8vo, cloth extra, 6s. Several Illustrations. (Rose Library, 2 vols., 1s. each.)

———— *Shawl Straps.* Small post 8vo, cloth extra, gilt, 3s. 6d.

———— *Eight Cousins; or, the Aunt Hill.* Small post 8vo, with Illustrations, 3s. 6d.

———— *The Rose in Bloom.* Small post 8vo, cloth extra, 3s. 6d.

———— *Silver Pitchers.* Small post 8vo, cloth extra, 3s. 6d.

———— *Under the Lilacs.* Small post 8vo, cloth extra, 5s.

"Miss Alcott's stories are thoroughly healthy, full of racy fun and humour . . . exceedingly entertaining . . . . We can recommend the 'Eight Cousins.'"—*Athenæum.*

Alpine Ascents and Adventures; or, Rock and Snow Sketches. By H. Schütz Wilson, of the Alpine Club. With Illustrations by Whymper and Marcus Stone. Crown 8vo, 10s. 6d. 2nd Edition.

Andersen (Hans Christian) Fairy Tales. With Illustrations in Colours by E. V. B. Royal 4to, cloth, 25s.

Andrews (Dr.) Latin-English Lexicon. New Edition. Royal 8vo, 1670 pp., cloth extra, 18s.

Animals Painted by Themselves. Adapted from the French of Balzac, Georges Sands, &c., with 200 Illustrations by Grandville. 8vo, cloth extra, gilt, 10s. 6d.

Art Education. See "Illustrated Text Books."

Art of Reading Aloud (The) in Pulpit, Lecture Room, or Private Reunions, with a perfect system of Economy of Lung Power on just principles for acquiring ease in Delivery, and a thorough command of the Voice. By G. Vandenhoff, M.A. Crown 8vo, cloth extra, 6s.

Art Treasures in the South Kensington Museum. Preparing for Publication in Monthly Parts, with the sanction of the Science and Art Department, each containing Many Plates price 1s. In this series will be included representations of Decorative Art of all countries and all times from objects in the South Kensington Museum, under the following classes :—

> Sculpture : Works in Marble, Ivory, and Terra-Cotta.
> Bronzes : Statuettes, Medallions, Plaques, Coins.
> Decorative Painting and Mosaic.
> Decorative Furniture and Carved Wood-Work.
> Ecclesiastical Metal-Work.
> Gold and Silversmiths' Work and Jewellery.
> Limoges and Oriental Enamels.
> Pottery of all Countries.
> Glass : Oriental, Venetian, and German.
> Ornamental Iron-Work : Cutlery.
> Textile Fabrics : Embroidery and Lace.
> Decorative Bookbinding.
> Original Designs for Works of Decorative Art.
> Views of the Courts and Galleries of the Museum.
> Architectural Decorations of the Museum.

The Plates will be carefully printed with a Japanese tint in atlas 8vo (13 in. by 9 in.), on thick ivory-tinted paper. They will be included in a stout wrapper, ornamented with a drawing from "The Genoa Doorway" recently acquired by the Museum.

Parts I. and II. are in preparation, and will be ready at Christmas.

Asiatic Turkey: being a Narrative of a Journey from Bombay to the Bosphorus, embracing a ride of over One Thousand Miles, from the head of the Persian Gulf to Antioch on the Mediterranean. By GRATTAN GEARY, Editor of the *Times of India.* 2 vols., crown 8vo, cloth extra, with many Illustrations, and a Route Map.

Atlantic Islands as Resorts of Health and Pleasure. By S. G. W. BENJAMIN, Author of "Contemporary Art in Europe," &c. Royal 8vo, cloth extra, with upwards of 150 Illustrations, 16s.

Australian Abroad (The). Branches from the Main Routes Round the World. Comprising the Author's Route through Japan, China, Cochin-China, Malasia, Sunda, Java, Torres Straits, Northern Australia, New South Wales, South Australia, and New Zealand. By JAMES HINGSTON ("J. H." of the *Melbourne Argus*). With Maps and numerous Illustrations from Photographs, including a Frontispiece, representing the famous Boer Buddha Temple, Java. Demy 8vo, 14s.

Autobiography of Sir G. Gilbert Scott, R.A., F.S.A., &c. Edited by his Son, G. GILBERT SCOTT. With an Introduction by the DEAN OF CHICHESTER, and a Funeral Sermon, preached in Westminster Abbey, by the DEAN OF WESTMINSTER. Also, Portrait on steel from the portrait of the Author by G. RICHMOND, R.A. 1 vol., demy 8vo, cloth extra, 18s.

B*AKER (Lieut.-Gen. Valentine, Pasha). See* "War in Bulgaria."

THE BAYARD SERIES,

Edited by the late J. HAIN FRISWELL.

Comprising Pleasure Books of Literature produced in the Choicest Style as Companionable Volumes at Home and Abroad.

"We can hardly imagine better books for boys to read or for men to ponder over."—*Times.*

Price 2s. 6d. each Volume, complete in itself, flexible cloth extra, gilt edges, with silk Headbands and Registers.

The Story of the Chevalier Bayard. By M. DE BERVILLE.

De Joinville's St. Louis, King of France.

The Essays of Abraham Cowley, including all his Prose Works.

Abdallah ; or the Four Leaves. By EDOUARD LABOULLAYE.

Table-Talk and Opinions of Napoleon Buonaparte.

Vathek: An Oriental Romance. By WILLIAM BECKFORD.

The Bayard Series (continued) :—

The King and the Commons. A Selection of Cavalier and
Puritan Songs. Edited by Prof. MORLEY.

Words of Wellington: *Maxims and Opinions of the Great*
Duke.

Dr. Johnson's Rasselas, Prince of Abyssinia. With Notes.

Hazlitt's Round Table. With Biographical Introduction.

The Religio Medici, Hydriotaphia, and the Letter to a Friend.
By Sir THOMAS BROWNE, Knt.

Ballad Poetry of the Affections. By ROBERT BUCHANAN.

Coleridge's Christabel, and other Imaginative Poems. With
Preface by ALGERNON C. SWINBURNE.

Lord Chesterfield's Letters, Sentences, and Maxims. With
Introduction by the Editor, and Essay on Chesterfield by M. DE STE.-
BEUVE, of the French Academy.

Essays in Mosaic. By THOS. BALLANTYNE.

My Uncle Toby; his Story and his Friends. Edited by
P. FITZGERALD.

Reflections; or, Moral Sentences and Maxims of the Duke de
la Rochefoucauld.

Socrates: Memoirs for English Readers from Xenophon's Memo-
rabilia. By EDW. LEVIEN.

Prince Albert's Golden Precepts.

A Case containing 12 Volumes, price 31s. 6d.; or the Case separately, price 3s. 6d.

Beauty and the Beast. An Old Tale retold, with Pictures by
E. V. B. Demy 4to, cloth extra, novel binding. 10 Illustrations
in Colours. 12s. 6d.

Beumers' German Copybooks. In six gradations at 4d. each.

Biart (Lucien). See "Adventures of a Young Naturalist,"
"My Rambles in the New World," "The Two Friends," "Involuntary Voyage"

Bickersteth's Hymnal Companion to Book of Common Prayer
may be had in various styles and bindings from 1d. to 21s. *Price
List and Prospectus will be forwarded on application.*

Bickersteth (Rev. E. H., M.A.) The Reef and other Parables.
1 vol., square 8vo, with numerous very beautiful Engravings, 2s. 6d.

——— *The Clergyman in his Home.* Small post 8vo, 1s.

——— *The Master's Home-Call; or, Brief Memorials of*
Alice Frances Bickersteth. 20th Thousand. 32mo, cloth gilt, 1s.

——— *The Master's Will.* A Funeral Sermon preached
on the Death of Mrs. S. Gurney Buxton. Sewn, 6d.; cloth gilt, 1s.

——— *The Shadow of the Rock.* A Selection of Religious
Poetry. 18mo, cloth extra, 2s. 6d.

Bickersteth (Rev. E. H., M.A.)   *The Shadowed Home and the* Light Beyond.   7th Edition, crown 8vo, cloth extra, 5*s.*

Bida.   *The Authorized Version of the Four Gospels,* with the whole of the magnificent Etchings on Steel, after drawings by M. BIDA, in 4 vols., appropriately bound in cloth extra, price 3*l.* 3*s.* each.

    Also the four volumes in two, bound in the best morocco, by Suttaby, extra gilt edges, 18*l.* 18*s.*, half-morocco, 12*l.* 12*s.*

    " Bida's Illustrations of the Gospels of St. Matthew and St. John have already received here and elsewhere a full recognition of their great merits."—*Times.*

Biographies of the Great Artists, Illustrated. This Series is issued in the form of Handbooks. Each is a Monograph of a Great Artist, and contains Portraits of the Masters, and as many examples of their art as can be readily procured. They are Illustrated with from 16 to 20 Full-page Engravings. Cloth, large crown 8vo, 3*s.* 6*d.* per Volume.

Titian.	**Rubens.**	**Tintoret and Veronese.**
Rembrandt.	**Lionardo.**	**Hogarth.**
Raphael.	**Turner.**	**Michelangelo.**
Van Dyck and Hals.	**The Little Masters.**	**Reynolds.**
Holbein.	**Delaroche & Vernet.**	**Gainsborough.**

Figure Painters of Holland.

    " A deserving Series, based upon recent German publications."—*Edinburgh Review.*

    " Most thoroughly and tastefully edited."—*Spectator.*

Black (Wm.) Three Feathers.   Small post 8vo, cloth extra, 6*s.*

———— *Lady Silverdale's Sweetheart, and other Stories.*   1 vol., small post 8vo, 6*s.*

———— *Kilmeny: a Novel.*   Small post 8vo, cloth, 6*s.*

———— *In Silk Attire.*   3rd Edition, small post 8vo, 6*s.*

———— *A Daughter of Heth.*   11th Edition, small post 8vo, 6*s.*

Blackmore (R. D.) Lorna Doone.   10th Edition, cr. 8vo, 6*s.*

————   " The reader at times holds his breath, so graphically yet so simply does John Ridd tell his tale."—*Saturday Review.*

———— *Alice Lorraine.*   1 vol., small post 8vo, 6th Edition, 6*s.*

———— *Clara Vaughan.*   Revised Edition, 6*s.*

———— *Cradock Nowell.*   New Edition, 6*s.*

———— *Cripps the Carrier.*   3rd Edition, small post 8vo, 6*s.*

———— *Mary Anerley.*   3 vols., 31*s.* 6*d.*   [*In the press.*

Blossoms from the King's Garden : Sermons for Children.   By the Rev. C. BOSANQUET. 2nd Edition, small post 8vo, cloth extra, 6*s.*

Blue Banner (The); or, The Adventures of a Mussulman, a Christian, and a Pagan, in the time of the Crusades and Mongol Conquest. Translated from the French of LEON CAHUN. With Seventy-six Wood Engravings. Square imperial 16mo, cloth, 7*s.* 6*d.*

Book of English Elegies. By W. F. MARCH PHILLIPPS. Small post 8vo, cloth extra, 5s.

Boy's Froissart (The). 7s. 6d. *See* "Froissart."

Brave Janet: A Story for Girls ; and, The Children's Trusts : A Story of Beech-Tree Dingle. By ALICE LEE. With Frontispiece by M. ELLEN EDWARDS. Square 8vo, cloth extra, 3s. 6d.

Brave Men in Action. By S. J. MACKENNA. Crown 8vo, 480 pp., cloth, 10s. 6d.

Brazil and the Brazilians. By J. C. FLETCHER and D. P. KIDDER. 9th Edition, Illustrated, 8vo, 21s.

Breton Folk : An Artistic Tour in Brittany. By HENRY BLACKBURN, Author of "Artists and Arabs," "Normandy Picturesque," &c. With 171 Illustrations by RANDOLPH CALDECOTT. Imperial 8vo, cloth extra, gilt edges, 21s.

British Goblins : Welsh Folk-Lore, Fairy Mythology, Legends, and Traditions. By WIRT SYKES, United States Consul for Wales. With Illustrations by J. H. THOMAS. This account of the Fairy Mythology and Folk-Lore of his Principality is, by permission, dedicated to His Royal Highness the Prince of Wales. 1 vol., demy 8vo, 18s.

Bryant (W. C., assisted by S. H. Gay) A Popular History of the United States. About 4 vols., to be profusely Illustrated with Engravings on Steel and Wood, after Designs by the best Artists. Vol. I., super-royal 8vo, cloth extra, gilt, 42s., is ready.

Buckle (Henry Thomas) The Life and Writings of. By ALFRED HENRY HUTH. With Portrait. 2 vols., demy 8vo.

Burnaby (Capt.) See "On Horseback."

Burnham Beeches (Heath, F. G.). With numerous Illustrations. Crown 8vo, cloth, gilt edges, 3s. 6d.

Butler (W. F.) The Great Lone Land; an Account of the Red River Expedition, 1869-70. With Illustrations and Map. Fifth and Cheaper Edition, crown 8vo, cloth extra, 7s. 6d.

────── *The Wild North Land ; the Story of a Winter Journey* with Dogs across Northern North America. Demy 8vo, cloth, with numerous Woodcuts and a Map, 4th Edition, 18s. Cr. 8vo, 7s. 6d.

────── *Akim-foo : the History of a Failure.* Demy 8vo, cloth, 2nd Edition, 16s. Also, in crown 8vo, 7s. 6d.

CADOGAN (Lady A.) Illustrated Games of Patience. Twenty-four Diagrams in Colours, with Descriptive Text. Foolscap 4to, cloth extra, gilt edges, 3rd Edition, 12s. 6d.

Caldecott (R.). See "Breton Folk."

Canada under the Administration of Lord Dufferin. By G. STEWART, Jun., Author of "Evenings in the Library," &c. Cloth gilt, 8vo, 15s.

Carbon Process (A Manual of). See LIESEGANG.

Ceramic Art. See JACQUEMART.

Changed Cross (The), and other Religious Poems. 16mo, 2*s.* 6*d.*

Chant Book Companion to the Book of Common Prayer. Consisting of upwards of 550 Chants for the Daily Psalms and for the Canticles ; also Kyrie Eleisons, and Music for the Hymns in Holy Communion, &c. Compiled and Arranged under the Musical Editorship of C. J. VINCENT, Mus. Bac. Crown 8vo, 2*s.* 6*d.* ; Organist's Edition, fcap. 4to, 5*s.*

Of various Editions of HYMNAL COMPANION, *Lists will be forwarded on application.*

Child of the Cavern (The) ; or, Strange Doings Underground. By JULES VERNE. Translated by W. H. G. KINGSTON. Numerous Illustrations. Sq. cr. 8vo, gilt edges, 7*s.* 6*d.* ; cl., plain edges, 5*s.*

Child's Play, with 16 Coloured Drawings by E. V. B. Printed on thick paper, with tints, 7*s.* 6*d.*

———— *New.* By E. V. B. Similar to the above. *See* New.

Children's Lives and How to Preserve Them ; or, The Nursery Handbook. By W. LOMAS, M.D. Crown 8vo, cloth, 5*s.*

Choice Editions of Choice Books. 2*s.* 6*d.* each, Illustrated by C. W. COPE, R.A., T. CRESWICK, R.A., E. DUNCAN, BIRKET FOSTER, J. C. HORSLEY, A.R.A., G. HICKS, R. REDGRAVE, R.A., C. STONEHOUSE, F. TAYLER, G. THOMAS, H. J. TOWNSHEND, E. H. WEHNERT, HARRISON WEIR, &c.

Bloomfield's Farmer's Boy.
Campbell's Pleasures of Hope.
Coleridge's Ancient Mariner.
Goldsmith's Deserted Village.
Goldsmith's Vicar of Wakefield.
Gray's Elegy in a Churchyard.
Keat's Eve of St. Agnes.

Milton's L'Allegro.
Poetry of Nature. Harrison Weir.
Rogers' (Sam.) Pleasures of Memory.
Shakespeare's Songs and Sonnets.
Tennyson's May Queen.
Elizabethan Poets.
Wordsworth's Pastoral Poems.

" Such works are a glorious beatification for a poet."—*Athenæum.*

Cobbett (William). A Biography. By EDWARD SMITH. 2 vols., crown 8vo, 25*s.*

Continental Tour of Eight Days for Forty-four Shillings. By a JOURNEY-MAN. 12mo, 1*s.*

" The book is simply delightful."—*Spectator.*

Covert Side Sketches : Thoughts on Hunting, with Different Packs in Different Countries. By J. NEVITT FITT (H.H. of the *Sporting Gazette,* late of the *Field*). 2nd Edition. Crown 8vo, cloth, 10*s.* 6*d.*

Cripps the Carrier. 3rd Edition, 6*s.* *See* BLACKMORE.

Cruise of H.M.S. " Challenger" (The). By W. J. J. SPRY, R.N. With Route Map and many Illustrations. 6th Edition, demy 8vo, cloth, 18*s.* Cheap Edition, crown 8vo, small type, some of the Illustrations, 7*s.* 6*d.*

Curious Adventures of a Field Cricket. By Dr. ERNEST CANDÈZE. Translated by N. D'ANVERS. With numerous fine Illustrations. Crown 8vo, cloth extra, gilt edges, 7*s.* 6*d.*

DANA (R. H.) Two Years before the Mast and Twenty-Four years After. Revised Edition with Notes, 12mo, 6s.

Daughter (A) of Heth. By W. BLACK. Crown 8vo, 6s.

Day of My Life (A) ; or, Every Day Experiences at Eton. By an ETON BOY, Author of "About Some Fellows." 16mo, cloth extra, 2s. 6d. 6th Thousand.

Day out of the Life of a Little Maiden (A): Six Studies from Life. By SHERER and ENGLER. Large 4to, in portfolio, 5s.

Diane. By Mrs. MACQUOID. Crown 8vo, 6s.

Dick Sands, the Boy Captain. By JULES VERNE. With nearly 100 Illustrations, cloth extra, gilt edges, 10s. 6d.

Discoveries of Prince Henry the Navigator, and their Results ; being the Narrative of the Discovery by Sea, within One Century, of more than Half the World. By RICHARD HENRY MAJOR, F.S.A. Demy 8vo, with several Woodcuts, 4 Maps, and a Portrait of Prince Henry in Colours. Cloth extra, 15s.

Dodge (Mrs. M.) Hans Brinker; or, the Silver Skates. An entirely New Edition, with 59 Full-page and other Woodcuts. Square crown 8vo, cloth extra, 7s. 6d. ; Text only, paper, 1s.

Dogs of Assize. A Legal Sketch-Book in Black and White. Containing 6 Drawings by WALTER J. ALLEN. Folio, in wrapper, 6s. 8d.

Dougall's (J. D.) Shooting; which see. 10s. 6d.

EARLY History of the Colony of Victoria (The), from its Discovery. By F. P. LABILLIERE. 2 vols., crown 8vo, 21s.

Echoes of the Heart. See MOODY.

Eight Cousins. See ALCOTT.

Eldmuir: An Art-Story of Scottish Home-Life, Scenery, and Incident. By JACOB THOMPSON, Jun. Illustrated with Engravings after Paintings of JACOB THOMPSON. With an Introductory Notice by LLEWELLYNN JEWITT, F.S.A., &c. Demy 8vo, cloth extra, 14s.

Elinor Dryden. By Mrs. MACQUOID. Crown 8vo, 6s.

Embroidery (Handbook of). By L. HIGGIN. Edited by LADY MARIAN ALFORD, and published by authority of the Royal School of Art Needlework, and dedicated to their President, H.R.H. PRINCESS CHRISTIAN, of Schleswig-Holstein, Princess of Great Britain and Ireland. With 16 page Illustrations, many of them in Colour, by BURNE JONES, WALTER CRANE, WILLIAM MORRIS, GEORGE AITCHISON, FAIRFAX WADE, the Rev. SELWYN IMAGE, and Miss JEKYLL ; and Designs for Borders, &c., by Miss WEBSTER, Miss BURNSIDE, and Miss MARY HERBERT, of the Royal School of Art Needlework. Crown 8vo, 5s.

English Catalogue of Books (The). Published during 1863 to 1871 inclusive, comprising also important American Publications. 30*s.*
　*** Of the previous Volume, 1835 to 1862, very few remain on sale; as also of the Index Volume, 1837 to 1857.

——— *Supplements,* 1863, 1864, 1865, 3*s.* 6*d.* each; 1866, 1867, to 1879, 5*s.* each.

English Writers, Chapters for Self-Improvement in English Literature. By the Author of "The Gentle Life," 6*s.*; smaller edition, 2*s.* 6*d.*

Erchomenon; or, The Republic of Materialism. Small post 8vo, cloth.

Eton. See "Day of my Life," "Out of School," "About Some Fellows."

Evans (C.) Over the Hills and Far Away. By C. EVANS. One Volume, crown 8vo, cloth extra, 10*s.* 6*d.*

——— *A Strange Friendship.* Crown 8vo, cloth, 5*s.*

FAITH Gartney's Girlhood. By the Author of "The Gayworthy's." Fcap. with Coloured Frontispiece, 3*s.* 6*d.*

Family Prayers for Working Men. By the Author of "Steps to the Throne of Grace." With an Introduction by the Rev. E. H. BICKERSTETH, M.A. Cloth, 1*s.*; sewed, 6*d.*

Fern Paradise (The): A Plea for the Culture of Ferns. By F. G. HEATH. New Edition, entirely Rewritten, Illustrated with Eighteen full-page, numerous other Woodcuts, and Four Photographs, large post 8vo, 12*s.* 6*d.* In 12 Parts, sewn, 1*s.* each.

Fern World (The). By F. G. HEATH. Illustrated by Twelve Coloured Plates, giving complete Figures (Sixty-four in all) of every Species of British Fern, printed from Nature; by several full-page Engravings. Cloth, gilt, 6th Edition, 12*s.* 6*d.* In 12 parts, 1*s.* each.

Few (A) Hints on Proving Wills. Enlarged Edition, 1*s.*

First Steps in Conversational French Grammar. By F. JULIEN. Being an Introduction to "Petites Leçons de Conversation et de Grammaire," by the same Author. Fcap. 8vo, 128 pp., 1*s.*

Flooding of the Sahara (The). See MACKENZIE.

Food for the People; or, Lentils and other Vegetable Cookery. By E. E. ORLEBAR. Third Thousand. Small post 8vo, boards, 1*s.*

Footsteps of the Master. See STOWE (Mrs. BEECHER).

Four Lectures on Electric Induction. Delivered at the Royal Institution, 1878-9. By J. E. H. GORDON, B.A. Cantab. With numerous Illustrations. Cloth limp, square 16mo, 3*s.*

Foreign Countries and the British Colonies. Edited by F. S.
PULLING, M.A., Lecturer at Queen's College, Oxford, and formerly
Professor at the Yorkshire College, Leeds. A Series of small Volumes
descriptive of the principal Countries of the World by well-known
Authors, each Country being treated of by a Writer who from
Personal Knowledge is qualified to speak with authority on the Subject.
The Volumes will average 180 crown 8vo pages, will contain Maps,
and, in some cases, a few typical Illustrations.

HEADINGS OF SECTIONS.

General Description, Position, &c. ; Physical Geography and Geology,
Climate ; Fauna and Flora ; Detailed Description, Provinces, Towns,
&c. ; Ethnology, Language ; National Characteristics ; Government,
Institutions, Political Life ; Military Organization, &c. ; Religion ;
Agriculture and Commerce ; Resources and Industries ; Communica-
tions Internal and External ; Literature and the Arts ; Social Life ;
History (but only in as far as is absolutely necessary to explain the
Present Condition of the Country.

The following Volumes are in preparation :—

Denmark and Iceland.	Russia.	Canada.
Greece.	Persia.	Sweden and Norway.
Switzerland.	Japan.	The West Indies.
Austria.	Peru.	New Zealand.

Franc (Maude Jeane). The following form one Series, small
post 8vo, in uniform cloth bindings:—

——— *Emily's Choice.* 5s.

——— *Hall's Vineyard.* 4s.

——— *John's Wife : a Story of Life in South Australia.* 4s.

——— *Marian ; or, the Light of Some One's Home.* 5s.

——— *Silken Cords and Iron Fetters.* 4s.

——— *Vermont Vale.* 5s.

——— *Minnie's Mission.* 4s.

——— *Little Mercy.* 5s.

Froissart (The Boy's). Selected from the Chronicles of England, France, Spain, &c. By SIDNEY LANIER. The Volume will
be fully Illustrated. Crown 8vo, cloth, 7s. 6d.

Friswell (J. H.) Our Square Circle. 2 vols., crown 8vo, cloth,
21s.

*** This work, announced two or three years ago, but withdrawn
in consequence of the late Mr. J. Hain Friswell's long illness and
death, has now been prepared for the press by his daughter, Miss
Laura Friswell.

Funny Foreigners and Eccentric Englishmen. 16 coloured
comic Illustrations for Children. Fcap. folio, coloured wrapper, 4s.

GAMES of Patience. See CADOGAN.

Gentle Life (Queen Edition). 2 vols. in 1, small 4to, 10s. 6d.

THE GENTLE LIFE SERIES.

Price 6s. each ; or in calf extra, price 10s. 6d. ; Smaller Edition, cloth extra, 2s. 6d.

A Reprint of these Volumes (with the exception of "Familiar Words") has been issued in very neat limp cloth bindings at 2s. 6d. each.

The Gentle Life. Essays in aid of the Formation of Character of Gentlemen and Gentlewomen. 21st Edition.

"Deserves to be printed in letters of gold, and circulated in every house."—*Chambers' Journal.*

About in the World. Essays by Author of " The Gentle Life."

" It is not easy to open it at any page without finding some handy idea."—*Morning Post.*

Like unto Christ. A New Translation of Thomas à Kempis' " De Imitatione Christi." 2nd Edition.

" Could not be presented in a more exquisite form, for a more sightly volume was never seen."—*Illustrated London News.*

Familiar Words. An Index Verborum, or Quotation Handbook. Affording an immediate Reference to Phrases and Sentences that have become embedded in the English language. 3rd and enlarged Edition. 6s.

"The most extensive dictionary of quotation we have met with."—*Notes and Queries.*

Essays by Montaigne. Edited and Annotated by the Author of "The Gentle Life." With Portrait. 2nd Edition.

"We should be glad if any words of ours could help to bespeak a large circulation for this handsome attractive book."—*Illustrated Times.*

The Countess of Pembroke's Arcadia. Written by Sir PHILIP SIDNEY. Edited with Notes by Author of " The Gentle Life." 7s. 6d.

" All the best things are retained intact in Mr. Friswell's edition."—*Examiner.*

The Gentle Life. 2nd Series, 8th Edition.

" There is not a single thought in the volume that does not contribute in some measure to the formation of a true gentleman."—*Daily News.*

The Silent Hour: Essays, Original and Selected. By the Author of "The Gentle Life." 3rd Edition.

" All who possess 'The Gentle Life' should own this volume."—*Standard.*

Half-Length Portraits. Short Studies of Notable Persons. By J. HAIN FRISWELL. Small post 8vo, cloth extra, 6s.

Essays on English Writers, for the Self-improvement of Students in English Literature.

" To all who have neglected to read and study their native literature we would certainly suggest the volume before us as a fitting introduction."—*Examiner.*

Other People's Windows. By J. HAIN FRISWELL. 3rd Edition.

"The chapters are so lively in themselves, so mingled with shrewd views of human nature, so full of illustrative anecdotes, that the reader cannot fail to be amused."—*Morning Post.*

A Man's Thoughts. By J. HAIN FRISWELL.

German Primer. Being an Introduction to First Steps in German. By M. T. PREU. 2s. 6d.

Getting On in the World ; or, Hints on Success in Life. By W. MATHEWS, LL.D. Small post 8vo, cloth, 2s. 6d.; gilt edges, 3s. 6d.

Gilpin's Forest Scenery. Edited by F. G. HEATH. 1 vol., large post 8vo, with numerous Illustrations. Uniform with "The Fern World" and "Our Woodland Trees." 12s. 6d.

Gordon (J. E. H.). See "Four Lectures on. Electric Induction," " Physical Treatise on Electricity," &c.

Gouffé. The Royal Cookery Book. By JULES GOUFFÉ; translated and adapted for English use by ALPHONSE GOUFFÉ, Head Pastrycook to her Majesty the Queen. Illustrated with large plates printed in colours. 161 Woodcuts, 8vo, cloth extra, gilt edges, 2l. 2s.

—————— Domestic Edition, half-bound, 10s. 6d.

"By far the ablest and most complete work on cookery that has ever been submitted to the gastronomical world."—*Pall Mall Gazette.*

Gouraud (Mdlle.) Four Gold Pieces. Numerous Illustrations. Small post 8vo, cloth, 2s. 6d. *See also* Rose Library.

Government of M. Thiers. By JULES SIMON. Translated from the French. 2 vols., demy 8vo, cloth extra, 32s.

Gower (Lord Ronald) Handbook to the Art Galleries, Public and Private, of Belgium and Holland. 18mo, cloth, 5s.

—————— *The Castle Howard Portraits.* 2 vols., folio, cl. extra, 6l. 6s.

Greek Grammar. See WALLER.

Guizot's History of France. Translated by ROBERT BLACK. Super-royal 8vo, very numerous Full-page and other Illustrations. In 5 vols., cloth extra, gilt, each 24s.

"It supplies a want which has long been felt, and ought to be in the hands of all students of history."—*Times.*

"Three-fourths of M. Guizot's great work are now completed, and the 'History of France,' which was so nobly planned, has been hitherto no less admirably executed."—*From long Review of Vol. III. in the Times.*

"M. Guizot's main merit is this, that, in a style at once clear and vigorous, he sketches the essential and most characteristic features of the times and personages described, and seizes upon every salient point which can best illustrate and bring out to view what is most significant and instructive in the spirit of the age described." —*Evening Standard,* Sept. 23, 1874.

—————————————————— *Masson's School Edition.* The History' of France from the Earliest Times to the Outbreak of the Revolution ; abridged from the Translation by Robert Black, M.A., with Chronological Index, Historical and Genealogical Tables, &c. By Professor GUSTAVE MASSON, B.A., Assistant Master at Harrow School. With 24 full-page Portraits, and many other Illustrations. 1 vol., demy 8vo, 600 pp., cloth extra, 10s. 6d.

—————— *History of England.* In 3 vols. of about 500 pp. each, containing 60 to 70 Full-page and other Illustrations, cl. extra, gilt, 24s. each.

"For luxury of typography, plainness of print, and beauty of illustration, these volumes, of which but one has as yet appeared in English, will hold their own against any production of an age so luxurious as our own in everything, typography not excepted."—*Times.*

Guillemin. See "World of Comets."
Guyon (Mde.) Life. By UPHAM. 6th Edition, crown 8vo, 6s.

*H*ANDBOOK *to the Charities of London. See* LOW's.

────── *of Embroidery ; which see.*
────── *to the Principal Schools of England. See* PRACTICAL.

Half-Hours of Blind Man's Holiday ; or, Summer and Winter Sketches in Black & White. By W. W. FENN. 2 vols., cr. 8vo, 24s.

Half-Length Portraits. Short Studies of Notable Persons. By J. HAIN FRISWELL. Small post 8vo, 6s. ; Smaller Edition, 2s. 6d.

Hall (W. W.) How to Live Long; or, 1408 *Health Maxims,* Physical, Mental, and Moral. By W. W. HALL, A.M., M.D. Small post 8vo, cloth, 2s. Second Edition.

Hans Brinker ; or, the Silver Skates. See DODGE.

Happy Valley (The) : Sketches of Kashmir and the Kashmiris. By W. WAKEFIELD, M.D. With Map and Illustrations. Demy 8vo, cloth, 15s.

Heart of Africa. Three Years' Travels and Adventures in the Unexplored Regions of Central Africa, from 1868 to 1871. By Dr. GEORG SCHWEINFURTH. Numerous Illustrations, and large Map. 2 vols., crown 8vo, cloth, 15s.

Heath (F. G.). See "Fern World," "Fern Paradise," "Our Woodland Trees," "Trees and Ferns;" "Gilpin's Forest Scenery," "Burnham Beeches," &c.

Heber's (Bishop) Illustrated Edition of Hymns. With upwards of 100 beautiful Engravings. Small 4to, handsomely bound, 7s. 6d. Morocco, 18s. 6d. and 21s. An entirely New Edition.

Hector Servadac. See VERNE. 10s. 6d.

Heir of Kilfinnan (The). New Story by W. H. G. KINGSTON, Author of "Snoe Shoes and Canoes," "With Axe and Rifle," &c. With Illustrations. Cloth, gilt edges, 7s. 6d.

Henderson (A.) Latin Proverbs and Quotations ; with Translations and Parallel Passages, and a copious English Index. By ALFRED HENDERSON. Fcap. 4to, 530 pp., 10s. 6d.

History and Handbook of Photography. Translated from the French of GASTON TISSANDIER. Edited by J. THOMSON. Imperial 16mo, over 300 pages, 70 Woodcuts, and Specimens of Prints by the best Permanent Processes. Second Edition, with an Appendix by the late Mr. HENRY FOX TALBOT. Cloth extra, 6s.

History of a Crime (The) ; Deposition of an Eye-witness. By VICTOR HUGO. 4 vols., crown 8vo, 42s. Cheap Edition, 1 vol., 6s.

────── *England. See* GUIZOT.

────── *France. See* GUIZOT.

History of Russia. *See* RAMBAUD.

—— *Merchant Shipping.* *See* LINDSAY.

—— *United States.* *See* BRYANT.

—— *Ireland.* By STANDISH O'GRADY. Vol. I. ready, 7*s.* 6*d.*

—— *American Literature.* By M. C. TYLER. Vols. I. and II., 2 vols, 8vo, 24*s.*

History and Principles of Weaving by Hand and by Power. With several hundred Illustrations. By ALFRED BARLOW. Royal 8vo, cloth extra, 1*l.* 5*s.* Second Edition.

Hitherto. By the Author of "The Gayworthys." New Edition, cloth extra, 3*s.* 6*d.* Also, in Rose Library, 2 vols., 2*s.*

Hofmann (Carl). A Practical Treatise on the Manufacture of Paper in all its Branches. Illustrated by 110 Wood Engravings, and 5 large Folding Plates. In 1 vol., 4to, cloth ; about 400 pp., 3*l.* 13*s.* 6*d.*

Home of the Eddas. By C. G. LOCK. Demy 8vo, cloth, 16*s.*

How to Live Long. *See* HALL.

Hugo (Victor) "*Ninety-Three.*" Illustrated. Crown 8vo, 6*s.*

—— *Toilers of the Sea.* Crown 8vo. Illustrated, 6*s.* ; fancy boards, 2*s.* ; cloth, 2*s.* 6*d.* ; On large paper with all the original Illustrations, 10*s.* 6*d.*

—— *See* "History of a Crime."

Hundred Greatest Men (The). 8 vols., containing 15 to 20 Portraits each, 21*s.* each. See below.

"Messrs. SAMPSON LOW & Co. are about to issue an important 'International' work, entitled, 'THE HUNDRED GREATEST MEN ;' being the Lives and Portraits of the 100 Greatest Men of History, divided into Eight Classes, each Class to form a Monthly Quarto Volume. The Introductions to the volumes are to be written by recognized authorities on the different subjects, the English contributors being DEAN STANLEY, Mr. MATTHEW ARNOLD, Mr. FROUDE, and Professor MAX MÜLLER : in Germany, Professor HELMHOLTZ : in France, MM. TAINE and RENAN ; and in America, Mr. EMERSON. The Portraits are to be Reproductions from fine and rare Steel Engravings."—*Academy.*

Hygiene and Public Health (A Treatise on). Edited by A. H. BUCK, M.D. Illustrated by numerous Wood Engravings. In 2 royal 8vo vols., cloth, one guinea each.

Hymnal Companion to Book of Common Prayer. *See* BICKERSTETH.

ILLUSTRATED Text-Books of Art-Education. A Series of Monthly Volumes preparing for publication. Edited by EDWARD J. POYNTER, R.A., Director for Art, Science and Art Department.

*The first Volumes, large crown 8vo, cloth, 3*s.* 6*d.* each, will be issued in the following divisions, the two first in December :—*

PAINTING.

Classic and Italian. | **French and Spanish.**
German, Flemish, and Dutch. | **English and American.**

ARCHITECTURE.

Classic and Early Christian. | **Gothic, Renaissance, & Modern.**

SCULPTURE.

Classic and Oriental. | **Renaissance and Modern.**

ORNAMENT.

Decoration in Colour. | **Architectural Ornament.**

Illustrations of China and its People. By J. THOMPSON, F.R.G.S. Four Volumes, imperial 4to, each 3*l.* 3*s.*

In my Indian Garden. By PHIL ROBINSON. With a Preface by EDWIN ARNOLD, M.A., C.S.I., &c. Crown 8vo, limp cloth, 3*s.* 6*d.*

Involuntary Voyage (An). Showing how a Frenchman who abhorred the Sea was most unwillingly and by a series of accidents driven round the World. Numerous Illustrations. Square crown 8vo, cloth extra, 7*s.* 6*d.*

Irish Bar. Comprising Anecdotes, Bon-Mots, and Biographical Sketches of the Bench and Bar of Ireland. By J. RODERICK O'FLANAGAN, Barrister-at-Law. Crown 8vo, 12*s.* Second Edition.

JACQUEMART (A.) History of the Ceramic Art: Descriptive and Analytical Study of the Potteries of all Times and of all Nations. By ALBERT JACQUEMART. 200 Woodcuts by H. Catenacci and J. Jacquemart. 12 Steel-plate Engravings, and 1000 Marks and Monograms. Translated by Mrs. BURY PALLISER. In 1 vol., super-royal 8vo, of about 700 pp., cloth extra, gilt edges, 28*s.*

Jimmy's Cruise in the Pinafore. See ALCOTT.

KAFIRLAND: A Ten Months' Campaign. By FRANK N. STREATFIELD, Resident Magistrate in Kaffraria, and Commandant of Native Levies during the Kaffir War of 1878. Crown 8vo, cloth extra, 7*s.* 6*d.*

Keble Autograph Birthday Book (The). Containing on each left-hand page the date and a selected verse from Keble's hymns. Imperial 8vo, with 12 Floral Chromos, ornamental binding, gilt edges, 15*s.*

Khedive's Egypt (The); or, The old House of Bondage under New Masters. By EDWIN DE LEON. Illustrated. Demy 8vo, cloth extra, Third Edition, 18*s.* Cheap Edition, 8*s.* 6*d.*

King's Rifle (The): From the Atlantic to the Indian Ocean; Across Unknown Countries; Discovery of the Great Zambesi Affluents, &c. By Major SERPA PINTO. With 24 full-page and about 100 half-page and smaller Illustrations, 13 small Maps, and 1 large one. 1 vol., demy 8vo.

Kingston (*W. H. G.*).   *See* "Snow-Shoes."
―――― *Child of the Cavern.*
―――― *Two Supercargoes.*
―――― *With Axe and Rifle.*
―――― *Begum's Fortune.*
―――― *Heir of Kilfinnan.*
Koldewey (*Capt.*) *The Second North German Polar Expedition*
in the Year 1869-70. Edited and condensed by H. W. BATES.
Numerous Woodcuts, Maps, and Chromo-lithographs. Royal 8vo,
cloth extra, 1*l.* 15*s.*

*L*ADY *Silverdale's Sweetheart.*   6*s.*   *See* BLACK.

Land of Bolivar (*The*) ; *or, War, Peace, and Adventure in the*
Republic of Venezuela.   By J. M. SPENCE, F.R.G.S.   2 vols., demy
8vo, with numerous Woodcuts and Maps, 31*s.* 6*d.*   Second Edition.
Landseer Gallery (*The*).   Containing thirty-six Autotype Re-
productions of Engravings from the most important early works of Sir
EDWIN LANDSEER.   With a Memoir of the Artist's Life, and
Descriptions of the Plates.   Imperial 4to, cloth, gilt edges, 2*l.* 2*s.*

Lenten Meditations.   In Two Series, each complete in itself.
By the Rev. CLAUDE BOSANQUET, Author of "Blossoms from the
King's Garden." 16mo, cloth, First Series, 1*s.* 6*d.* ; Second Series, 2*s.*

Lentils.   *See* "Food for the People."

Liesegang (*Dr. Paul E.*) *A Manual of the Carbon Process of*
Photography.   Demy 8vo, half-bound, with Illustrations, 4*s.*

Life and Letters of the Honourable Charles Sumner (*The*).
2 vols., royal 8vo, cloth.   The Letters give full description of London
Society—Lawyers—Judges—Visits to Lords Fitzwilliam, Leicester,
Wharncliffe, Brougham—Association with Sydney Smith, Hallam,
Macaulay, Dean Milman, Rogers, and Talfourd ; also, a full Journal
which Sumner kept in Paris.   Second Edition, 36*s.*

Lindsay (*W. S.*) *History of Merchant Shipping and Ancient*
Commerce.   Over 150 Illustrations, Maps and Charts.   In 4 vols.,
demy 8vo, cloth extra.   Vols. 1 and 2, 21*s.* ; vols. 3 and 4, 24*s.* each.

Lion Jack : a Story of Perilous Adventures amongst Wild Men
and Beasts.   Showing how Menageries are made.   By P. T. BARNUM.
With Illustrations.   Crown 8vo, cloth extra, price 6*s.*

Little King ; or, the Taming of a Young Russian Count.   By
S. BLANDY.   64 Illustrations.   Crown 8vo, gilt, 7*s.* 6*d.*

Little Mercy ; or, For Better for Worse.   By MAUDE JEANNE
FRANC, Author of "Marian," "Vermont Vale," &c., &c.   Small
post 8vo, cloth extra, 4*s.*   Second Edition.

Long (Col. C. Chaillé) Central Africa. Naked Truths of Naked People : an Account of Expeditions to Lake Victoria Nyanza and the Mabraka Niam-Niam. Demy 8vo, numerous Illustrations, 18*s.*

Lost Sir Massingberd. New Edition, crown 8o, boards, coloured wrapper, 2*s.*

Low's German Series—

1. **The Illustrated German Primer.** Being the easiest introduction to the study of German for all beginners. 1*s.*
2. **The Children's own German Book.** A Selection of Amusing and Instructive Stories in Prose. Edited by Dr. A. L. MEISSNER. Small post 8vo, cloth, 1*s. 6d.*
3. **The First German Reader, for Children from Ten to** Fourteen. Edited by Dr. A. L. MEISSNER. Small post 8vo, cloth, 1*s. 6d.*
4. **The Second German Reader.** Edited by Dr. A. L. MEISSNER. Small post 8vo, cloth, 1*s. 6d.*

Buchheim's Deutsche Prosa. Two Volumes, sold separately :—

5. **Schiller's Prosa.** Containing Selections from the Prose Works of Schiller, with Notes for English Students. By Dr. BUCHHEIM, Small post 8vo, 2*s. 6d.*
6. **Goethe's Prosa.** Selections from the Prose Works of Goethe, with Notes for English Students. By Dr. BUCHHEIM. Small post 8vo, 3*s. 6d.*

Low's International Series of Toy Books. 6*d.* each ; or Mounted on Linen, 1*s.*

1. **Little Fred and his Fiddle,** from Asbjörnsen's "Norwegian Fairy Tales."
2. **The Lad and the North Wind,**   ditto.
3. **The Pancake,**   ditto.

(*The Series will be continued.*)

Low's Standard Library of Travel and Adventure. Crown 8vo, bound uniformly in cloth extra, price 7*s. 6d.*

1. **The Great Lone Land.** By W. F. BUTLER, C.B.
2. **The Wild North Land.** By W. F. BUTLER, C.B.
3. **How I found Livingstone.** By H. M. STANLEY.
4. **The Threshold of the Unknown Region.** By C. R. MARKHAM. (4th Edition, with Additional Chapters, 10*s. 6d.*)
5. **A Whaling Cruise to Baffin's Bay and the Gulf of Boothia.** By A. H. MARKHAM.

Low's Standard Library of Travel and Adventure, continued :—

6. **Campaigning on the Oxus.** By J. A. MACGAHAN.
7. **Akim-foo : the History of a Failure.** By MAJOR W. F. BUTLER, C.B.
8. **Ocean to Ocean.** By the Rev. GEORGE M. GRANT. With Illustrations.
9. **Cruise of the Challenger.** By W. J. J. SPRY, R.N.
10. **Schweinfurth's Heart of Africa.** 2 vols., 15*s.*
11. **Through the Dark Continent.** By H. M. STANLEY. 1 vol., 12*s. 6d.*

Low's Standard Novels. Crown 8vo, 6*s.* each, cloth extra.

Three Feathers. By WILLIAM BLACK.

A Daughter of Heth. 13th Edition. By W. BLACK. With Frontispiece by F. WALKER, A.R.A.

Kilmeny. A Novel. By W. BLACK.

In Silk Attire. By W. BLACK.

Lady Silverdale's Sweetheart. By W. BLACK.

Alice Lorraine. By R. D. BLACKMORE.

Lorna Doone. By R. D. BLACKMORE. 8th Edition.

Cradock Nowell. By R. D. BLACKMORE.

Clara Vaughan. By R. D. BLACKMORE.

Cripps the Carrier. By R. D. BLACKMORE.

Innocent. By Mrs. OLIPHANT. Eight Illustrations.

Work. A Story of Experience. By LOUISA M. ALCOTT. Illustrations. *See also* Rose Library.

A French Heiress in her own Chateau. By the author of " One Only," "Constantia," &c. Six Illustrations.

Ninety-Three. By VICTOR HUGO. Numerous Illustrations.

My Wife and I. By Mrs. BEECHER STOWE.

Wreck of the Grosvenor. By W. CLARK RUSSELL.

Elinor Dryden. By Mrs. MACQUOID.

Diane. By Mrs. MACQUOID.

Poganuc People, Their Loves and Lives. By Mrs. BEECHER STOWE.

Low's Handbook to the Charities of London for 1879. Edited and revised to July, 1879, by C. MACKESON, F.S.S., Editor of " A Guide to the Churches of London and its Suburbs," &c. 1*s.*

*M*ACGAHAN (*J. A.*) *Campaigning on the Oxus, and the* Fall of Khiva. With Map and numerous Illustrations, 4th Edition, small post 8vo, cloth extra, 7*s. 6d.*

Macgregor (John) " Rob Roy " on the Baltic. 3rd Edition, small post 8vo, 2s. 6d.

—— *A Thousand Miles in the "Rob Roy " Canoe.* 11th Edition, small post 8vo, 2s. 6d.

—— *Description of the " Rob Roy" Canoe,* with Plans, &c., 1s.

—— *The Voyage Alone in the Yawl " Rob Roy."* New Edition, thoroughly revised, with additions, small post 8vo, 5s.

Mackenzie (D). The Flooding of the Sahara. An Account of the Project for opening direct communication with 38,000,000 people. With a Description of North-West Africa and Soudan. By DONALD MACKENZIE. 8vo, cloth extra, with Illustrations, 10s. 6d.

Macquoid (Mrs.) Elinor Dryden. Crown 8vo, cloth, 6s.

—— *Diane.* Crown 8vo, 6s.

Marked Life (A) ; or, The Autobiography of a Clairvoyante. By "GIPSY." Post 8vo, 5s.

Markham (A. H.) The Cruise of the " Rosario." By A. H. MARKHAM, R.N. 8vo, cloth extra, with Map and Illustrations.

—— *A Whaling Cruise to Baffin's Bay and the Gulf of Boothia.* 3rd and Cheaper Edition, crown 8vo, 2 Maps and several Illustrations, cloth extra, 7s. 6d.

Markham (C. R.) The Threshold of the Unknown Region. Crown 8vo, with Four Maps, 4th Edition. Cloth extra, 10s. 6d.

Maury (Commander) Physical Geography of the Sea, and its Meteorology. Being a Reconstruction and Enlargement of his former Work, with Charts and Diagrams. New Edition, crown 8vo, 6s.

Memoirs of Madame de Rémusat, 1802—1808. By her Grandson, M. PAUL DE RÉMUSAT, Senator. Translated by Mrs. CASHEL HOEY and and Mr. JOHN LILLIE. 2 vols., demy 8vo, cloth extra. This work was written by Madame de Rémusat during the time she was living on the most intimate terms with the Empress Josephine, and is full of revelations respecting the private life of Bonaparte, and of men and politics of the first years of the century. Revelations which have already created a great sensation in Paris. Demy 8vo, 2 vols.

Men of Mark : a Gallery of Contemporary Portraits of the most Eminent Men of the Day taken from Life, especially for this publication, price 1s. 6d. monthly. Vols. I., II., and III. handsomely bound, cloth, gilt edges, 25s. each.

Michael Strogoff. 10s. 6d. and 5s. *See* VERNE.

Michie (Sir A., K.C.M.G.) See " Readings in Melbourne."

Mitford (Miss). See " Our Village."

Montaigne's Essays.   See "Gentle Life Series."

Moody (Emma) Echoes of the Heart.   A Collection of upwards of 200 Sacred Poems.   16mo, cloth, gilt edges, 3*s.* 6*d.*

My Brother Jack; or, The Story of Whatd'yecallem.   Written by Himself.   From the French of ALPHONSE DAUDET.   Illustrated by P. PHILIPPOTEAUX.   Square imperial 16mo, cloth extra, 7*s.* 6*d.*

My Rambles in the New World.   By LUCIEN BIART, Author of "The Adventures of a Young Naturalist."   Crown 8vo, cloth extra. Numerous full-page Illustrations, 7*s.* 6*d.*

Mysterious Island.   By JULES VERNE.   3 vols., imperial 16mo. 150 Illustrations, cloth gilt, 3*s.* 6*d.* each ; elaborately bound, gilt edges, 7*s.* 6*d.* each.

NARES (Sir G. S., K.C.B.) Narrative of a Voyage to the Polar Sea during 1875-76, in H.M.'s Ships "Alert" and "Discovery." By Captain Sir G. S. NARES, R.N., K.C.B., F.R.S.   Published by permission of the Lords Commissioners of the Admiralty.   With Notes on the Natural History, edited by H. W. FEILDEN, F.G.S., C.M.Z.S., F.R.G.S., Naturalist to the Expedition.   Two Volumes, demy 8vo, with numerous Woodcut Illustrations, Photographs, &c.   4th Edition, 2*l.* 2*s.*

National Music of the World.   By the late HENRY F. CHORLEY.   Edited by H. G. HEWLETT, Author of "Memoir of H. F. CHORLEY."   1 vol., crown 8vo, cloth.

"What I have to offer are not a few impressions, scrambled together in the haste of the moment, but are the result of many years of comparison and experience."— *From the Author's "Prelude."*

New Child's Play (A).   Sixteen Drawings by E. V. B.   Beautifully printed in colours, 4to, cloth extra, 12*s.* 6*d.*

New Guinea (A Few Months in).   By OCTAVIUS C. STONE, F.R.G.S.   With numerous Illustrations from the Author's own Drawings.   Crown 8vo, cloth, 12*s.*

*** Until the Author's own visit, no English explorer, except Wallace, had resided in that *terra incognita,* although it had been discovered 350 years before.

New Ireland.   By A. M. SULLIVAN, M.P. for Louth.   2 vols., demy 8vo, 30*s.*   Cheaper Edition, 1 vol., crown 8vo, 8*s.* 6*d.*

Noble Words and Noble Deeds.   Translated from the French of E. MULLER, by DORA LEIGH.   Containing many Full-page Illustrations by PHILIPPOTEAUX.   Square imperial 16mo, cloth extra, 7*s.* 6*d.*

"This is a book which will delight the young. . . . We cannot imagine a nicer present than this book for children."—*Standard.*
"Is certain to become a favourite with young people."—*Court Journal.*

North American Review (*The*).   Monthly, price 2s. 6d.

Notes on Fish and Fishing.   By the Rev. J. J. MANLEY, M.A.
With Illustrations, crown 8vo, cloth extra, leatherette binding, 10s. 6d.

Novels.   Crown 8vo, cloth, 10s. 6d. per vol. :—

Mary Anerley. By R. D. BLACKMORE, Author of "Lorna Doone,"
&c.   3 vols.   [*In the press.*

All the World's a Stage. By M. A. M. HOPPUS, Author of "Five
Chimnney Farm."   3 vols.

Cressida. By M. B. THOMAS.   3 vols.

A Woman of Mind.   3 vols.

The Cossacks. By COUNT TOLSTOY.   Translated from the Russian
by EUGENE SCHUYLER, Author of "Turkistan."   2 vols.

A Stroke of an Afghan Knife. By R. A. STERNDALE, F.R.G.S.,
Author of "Seonee."   3 vols.

The Braes of Yarrow. By C. GIBBON.   3 vols.

Auld Lang Syne. By the Author of "The Wreck of the Grosvenor."
2 vols.

On the Wolds. By the Rev. E. GILLIAT, Author of "Asylum
Christi."   2 vols.

In a Rash Moment. By JESSIE McLAREN.   2 vols.

Old Charlton. By BADEN PRITCHARD.   3 vols.

Our Square Circle. By the late J. D. FRISWELL.   2 vols.

Nursery Playmates (*Prince of*).   217 Coloured pictures for
Children by eminent Artists.   Folio, in coloured boards, 6s.

*O*CEAN *to Ocean : Sandford Fleming's Expedition through*
Canada in 1872.   By the Rev. GEORGE M. GRANT.   With Illustrations.   Revised and enlarged Edition, crown 8vo, cloth, 7s. 6d.

Old-Fashioned Girl.   See ALCOTT.

Oliphant (*Mrs.*) *Innocent.*   A Tale of Modern Life.   By Mrs
OLIPHANT, Author of "The Chronicles of Carlingford," &c., &c.
With Eight Full-page Illustrations, small post 8vo, cloth extra, 6s.

On Horseback through Asia Minor.   By Capt. FRED BURNABY,
Royal Horse Guards, Author of "A Ride to Khiva."   2 vols.,
8vo, with three Maps and Portrait of Author, 6th Edition, 38s. ;
Cheaper Edition, crown 8vo, 10s. 6d.

Our Little Ones in Heaven.   Edited by the Rev. H. ROBBINS.
With Frontispiece after Sir JOSHUA REYNOLDS.   Fcap., cloth extra,
New Edition—the 3rd, with Illustrations, 5s.

Our Village. By Mary Russell Mitford. Illustrated with Frontispiece Steel Engraving, and 12 full-page and 157 smaller Cuts of Figure Subjects and Scenes, from Drawings by W. H. J. Boot and C. O. Murray. Chiefly from Sketches made by these Artists in the neighbourhood of "Our Village." Crown 4to, cloth, gilt edges, 21*s.*

Our Woodland Trees. By F. G. Heath. Large post 8vo, cloth, gilt edges, uniform with "Fern World" and "Fern Paradise," by the same Author. 8 Coloured Plates and 20 Woodcuts, 12*s.* 6*d.*

Out of School at Eton. Being a collection of Poetry and Prose Writings. By Some Present Etonians. Foolscap 8vo, cloth, 3*s.* 6*d.*

PAINTERS of All Schools. By Louis Viardot, and other Writers. 500 pp., super-royal 8vo, 20 Full-page and 70 smaller Engravings, cloth extra, 25*s.* A New Edition is being issued in Half-crown parts, with fifty additional portraits, cloth, gilt edges, 31*s.* 6*d.*

"A handsome volume, full of information and sound criticism."—*Times.*
"Almost an encyclopædia of painting. . . . . It may be recommended as a handy and elegant guide to beginners in the study of the history of art."—*Saturday Review.*

Palliser (Mrs.) A History of Lace, from the Earliest Period. A New and Revised Edition, with additional cuts and text, upwards of 100 Illustrations and coloured Designs. 1 vol. 8vo, 1*l.* 1*s.*

"One of the most readable books of the season ; permanently valuable, always interesting, often amusing, and not inferior in all the essentials of a gift book."—*Times.*

——— *Historic Devices, Badges, and War Cries.* 8vo, 1*l.* 1*s.*

——— *The China Collector's Pocket Companion.* With upwards of 1000 Illustrations of Marks and Monograms. 2nd Edition, with Additions. Small post 8vo, limp cloth, 5*s.*

Petites Leçons de Conversation et de Grammaire: Oral and Conversational Method ; being Little Lessons introducing the most Useful Topics of Daily Conversation, upon an entirely new principle, &c. By F. Julien, French Master at King Edward the Sixth's Grammar School, Birmingham. Author of "The Student's French Examiner," "First Steps in Conversational French Grammar," which see.

Phillips (L.) Dictionary of Biographical Reference. 8vo, 1*l.* 11*s.* 6*d.*

Photography (History and Handbook of). See Tissandier.

Physical Treatise on Electricity and Magnetism. By J. E. H. Gordon, B.A. One volume, demy 8vo, very numerous Illustrations. Among the newer portions of the work may be enumerated : All the more recent investigations on Striæ by Spottiswoode, De la Rue, Moulton, &c. An account of Mr. Crooke's recent researches. Full descriptions and pictures of all the modern Magnetic Survey Instruments now used at Kew Observatory. Full accounts of all the modern work on Specific Inductive Capacity. Full accounts of the more recent determination of the ratio of Electric units (v). It is believed that in respect to the number and beauty of the Illustrations, the work will be quite unique.

Picture Gallery of British Art (The). 38 Permanent Photographs after the most celebrated English Painters. With Descriptive Letterpress. Vols. 1 to 5, cloth extra, 18*s.* each. Vol. 6 for 1877, commencing New Series, demy folio, 31*s.* 6*d.* Monthly Parts, 1*s.* 6*d.*

Pinto (Major Serpa). See " King's Rifle."

Placita Anglo-Normannica. The Procedure and Constitution of the Anglo-Norman Courts (WILLIAM I.—RICHARD I.), as shown by Contemporaneous Records ; all the Reports of the Litigation of the period, as recorded in the Chronicles and Histories of the time, being gleaned and literally transcribed. With Explanatory Notes, &c. By M. M. BIGELOW. Demy 8vo, cloth, 21*s.*

Plutarch's Lives. An Entirely New and Library Edition. Edited by A. H. CLOUGH, Esq. 5 vols., 8vo, 2*l.* 10*s.* ; half-morocco, gilt top, 3*l.* Also in 1 vol., royal 8vo, 800 pp., cloth extra, 18*s.* ; half-bound, 21*s.*

—— *Morals.* Uniform with Clough's Edition of " Lives of Plutarch." Edited by Professor GOODWIN. 5 vols., 8vo, 3*l.* 3*s.*

Poe (E. A.) The Works of. 4 vols., 2*l.* 2*s.*

Poems of the Inner Life. A New Edition, Revised, with many additional Poems. Small post 8vo, cloth, 5*s.*

Poganuc People: their Loves and Lives. By Mrs. BEECHER STOWE. Crown 8vo, cloth, 6*s.*

Polar Expeditions. See KOLDEWEY, MARKHAM, MACGAHAN and NARES.

Pottery: how it is Made, its Shape and Decoration. Practical Instructions for Painting on Porcelain and all kinds of Pottery with vitrifiable and common Oil Colours. By G. WARD NICHOLS. 42 Illustrations, crown 8vo, red edges, 6*s.*

Practical (A) Handbook to the Principal Schools of England. By C. E. PASCOE. New Edition corrected to 1879, crown 8vo, cloth extra, 3*s.* 6*d.*

"This is an exceedingly useful work, and one that was much wanted."—*Examiner.*

Prejevalsky (N. M.) From Kulja, across the Tian Shan to Lob- nor. Translated by E. DELMAR MORGAN, F.R.G.S. With Notes and Introduction by SIR DOUGLAS FORSYTH, K.C.S.I. 1 vol., demy 8vo, with a Map. 16*s.*

Prince Ritto ; or, The Four-leaved Shamrock. By FANNY W. CURREY. With 10 Full-page Fac-simile Reproductions of Original Drawings by HELEN O'HARA. Demy 4to, cloth extra, gilt, 10s. 6d.

Publishers' Circular (The), and General Record of British and Foreign Literature. Published on the 1st and 15th of every Month.

QUARTER Sessions, from Queen Elizabeth to Queen Anne: Illustrations of Local Government and History. Drawn from Original Records (chiefly of the County of Devon). By A. H. A. HAMILTON. Crown 8vo, cloth, 10s. 6d.

RAMBAUD (Alfred). History of Russia, from its Origin in the Year 1877. With Six Maps. Translated by Mrs. L. B. LANG. 2 vols., demy 8vo, cloth extra, 38s.

Mr. W. R. S. Ralston, in the *Academy*, says, "We gladly recognize in the present volume a trustworthy history of Russia."

"We will venture to prophecy that it will become *the* work on the subject for readers in our part of Europe. . . . Mrs. Lang has done her work remarkably well."—*Athenæum.*

Readings in Melbourne ; with an Essay on the Resources and Prospects of Victoria for the Emigrant and Uneasy Classes. By Sir ARCHIBALD MICHIE, Q.C., K.C.M.G., Agent-General for Victoria. With Coloured Map of Australia. Crown 8vo, cloth extra, price 7s. 6d.

Recollections of Writers. By CHARLES and MARY COWDEN CLARKE. Authors of "The Concordance to Shakespeare," &c. ; with Letters of CHARLES LAMB, LEIGH HUNT, DOUGLAS JERROLD, and CHARLES DICKENS ; and a Preface by MARY COWDEN CLARKE. Crown 8vo, cloth, 10s. 6d.

Reminiscences of the War in New Zealand. By THOMAS W. GUDGEON, Lieutenant and Quartermaster, Colonial Forces, N.Z. With Twelve Portraits. Crown 8vo, cloth extra, 10s. 6d.

Rémusat (Madame de). See "Memoirs of."

Robinson (Phil.). See "In my Indian Garden."

Rochefoucauld's Reflections. Bayard Series, 2s. 6d.

Rogers (S.) Pleasures of Memory. See "Choice Editions of Choice Books." 2s. 6d.

Rose in Bloom. See ALCOTT.

Rose Library (The). Popular Literature of all countries. Each volume, 1s. ; cloth, 2s. 6d. Many of the Volumes are Illustrated—

1. **Sea-Gull Rock.** By JULES SANDEAU. Illustrated.
2. **Little Women.** By LOUISA M. ALCOTT.
3. **Little Women Wedded.** Forming a Sequel to "Little Women."
4. **The House on Wheels.** By MADAME DE STOLZ. Illustrated.
5. **Little Men.** By LOUISA M. ALCOTT. Dble. vol., 2s. ; cloth, 3s. 6d.

The Rose Library, continued :—

6. **The Old-Fashioned Girl.** By LOUISA M. ALCOTT. Double vol., 2*s.* ; cloth, 3*s.* 6*d.*

7. **The Mistress of the Manse.** By J. G. HOLLAND.

8. **Timothy Titcomb's Letters to Young People, Single and Married.**

9. **Undine, and the Two Captains.** By Baron DE LA MOTTE FOUQUÉ. A New Translation by F. E. BUNNETT. Illustrated.

10. **Draxy Miller's Dowry, and the Elder's Wife.** By SAXE HOLM.

11. **The Four Gold Pieces.** By Madame GOURAUD. Numerous Illustrations.

12. **Work.** A Story of Experience. First Portion. By LOUISA M. ALCOTT.

13. **Beginning Again.** Being a Continuation of "Work." By LOUISA M. ALCOTT.

14. **Picciola; or, the Prison Flower.** By X. B. SAINTINE. Numerous Graphic Illustrations.

15. **Robert's Holidays.** Illustrated.

16. **The Two Children of St. Domingo.** Numerous Illustrations.

17. **Aunt Jo's Scrap Bag.**

18. **Stowe (Mrs. H. B.) The Pearl of Orr's Island.**

19. ———— **The Minister's Wooing.**

20. ———— **Betty's Bright Idea.**

21. ———— **The Ghost in the Mill.**

22. ———— **Captain Kidd's Money.**

23. ———— **We and our Neighbours.** Double vol., 2*s.*

24. ———— **My Wife and I.** Double vol., 2*s.* ; cloth, gilt, 3*s.* 6*d.*

25. **Hans Brinker ; or, the Silver Skates.**

26. **Lowell's My Study Window.**

27. **Holmes (O. W.) The Guardian Angel.**

28. **Warner (C. D.) My Summer in a Garden.**

29. **Hitherto.** By the Author of "The Gayworthys." 2 vols., 1*s.* each.

30. **Helen's Babies.** By their Latest Victim.

31. **The Barton Experiment.** By the Author of "Helen's Babies."

32. **Dred.** By Mrs. BEECHER STOWE. Double vol., 2*s.* Cloth, gilt, 3*s.* 6*d.*

33. **Warner (C. D.) In the Wilderness.**

34. **Six to One.** A Seaside Story.

Russell (W. H., LL.D.) The Tour of the Prince of Wales in India. By W. H. RUSSELL, LL.D. Fully Illustrated by SYDNEY P. HALL, M.A. Super-royal 8vo, cloth extra, gilt edges, 52*s.* 6*d.*; Large Paper Edition, 84*s.*

SANCTA Christina: a Story of the First Century. By ELEANOR E. ORLEBAR. With a Preface by the Bishop of Winchester. Small post 8vo, cloth extra, 5*s.*

Scientific Memoirs: being Experimental Contributions to a Knowledge of Radiant Energy. By JOHN WILLIAM DRAPER, M.D., LL.D., Author of "A Treatise on Human Physiology," &c. With Steel Portrait of the Author. Demy 8vo, cloth, 473 pages, 14*s.*

Scott (Sir G. Gilbert.) *See* " Autobiography."

Sea-Gull Rock. By JULES SANDEAU, of the French Academy. Royal 16mo, with 79 Illustrations, cloth extra, gilt edges, 7*s. 6d.* Cheaper Edition, cloth gilt, 2*s. 6d.* *See also* Rose Library.

Seonee: Sporting in the Satpura Range of Central India, and in the Valley of the Nerbudda. By R. A. STERNDALE, F.R.G.S. 8vo, with numerous Illustrations, 21*s.*

Shakespeare (The Boudoir). Edited by HENRY CUNDELL. Carefully bracketted for reading aloud ; freed from all objectionable matter, and altogether free from notes. Price 2*s. 6d.* each volume, cloth extra, gilt edges. Contents :—Vol I., Cymbeline—Merchant of Venice. Each play separately, paper cover, 1*s.* Vol. II., As You Like It—King Lear—Much Ado about Nothing. Vol. III., Romeo and Juliet—Twelfth Night—King John. The latter six plays separately, paper cover, 9*d.*

Shakespeare Key (The). Forming a Companion to "The Complete Concordance to Shakespeare." By CHARLES and MARY COWDEN CLARKE. Demy 8vo, 800 pp., 21*s.*

Shooting: its Appliances, Practice, and Purpose. By JAMES DALZIEL DOUGALL, F.S.A., F.Z.A. Author of "Scottish Field Sports," &c. Crown 8vo, cloth extra, 10*s. 6d.*

"The book is admirable in every way. . . . . We wish it every success."—*Globe.*
"A very complete treatise. . . . . Likely to take high rank as an authority on shooting."—*Daily News.*

Silent Hour (The). *See* "Gentle Life Series."

Silver Pitchers. *See* ALCOTT.

Simon (Jules). *See* " Government of M. Thiers."

Six to One. A Seaside Story. 16mo, boards, 1*s.*

Sketches from an Artist's Portfolio. By SYDNEY P. HALL. About 60 Fac-similes of his Sketches during Travels in various parts of Europe. Folio, cloth extra, 3*l.* 3*s.*

"A portfolio which any one might be glad to call their own."—*Times.*

Sleepy Sketches ; or, How we Live, and How we Do Not Live. From Bombay. 1 vol., small post 8vo, cloth, 6*s.*

"Well-written and amusing sketches of Indian society."—*Morning Post.*

Smith (G.) Assyrian Explorations and Discoveries. By the late GEORGE SMITH. Illustrated by Photographs and Woodcuts. Demy 8vo, 6th Edition, 18s.

———— *The Chaldean Account of Genesis.* By the late G. SMITH, of the Department of Oriental Antiquities, British Museum. With many Illustrations. Demy 8vo, cloth extra, 6th Edition, 16s.

Snow-Shoes and Canoes; or, the Adventures of a Fur-Hunter in the Hudson's Bay Territory. By W. H. G. KINGSTON. 2nd Edition. With numerous Illustrations. Square crown 8vo, cloth extra, gilt, 7s. 6d.

Songs and Etchings in Shade and Sunshine. By J. E. G. Illustrated with 44 Etchings. Small 4to, cloth, gilt tops, 25s.

South Kensington Museum. See " Art Treasures."

Stanley (H. M.) How I Found Livingstone. Crown 8vo, cloth extra, 7s. 6d. ; large Paper Edition, 10s. 6d.

———— *" My Kalulu," Prince, King, and Slave.* A Story from Central Africa. Crown 8vo, about 430 pp., with numerous graphic Illustrations, after Original Designs by the Author. Cloth, 7s. 6d.

———— *Coomassie and Magdala.* A Story of Two British Campaigns in Africa. Demy 8vo, with Maps and Illustrations, 16s.

———— *Through the Dark Continent,* which see.

St. Nicholas Magazine. 1s. monthly.

Story without an End. From the German of Carové, by the late Mrs. SARAH T. AUSTIN. Crown 4to, with 15 Exquisite Drawings by E. V. B., printed in Colours in Fac-simile of the original Water Colours ; and numerous other Illustrations. New Edition, 7s. 6d.

———— square 4to, with Illustrations by HARVEY. 2s. 6d.

Stowe (Mrs. Beecher) Dred. Cheap Edition, boards, 2s. Cloth, gilt edges, 3s. 6d.

———— *Footsteps of the Master.* With Illustrations and red borders. Small post 8vo, cloth extra, 6s.

———— *Geography,* with 60 Illustrations. Square cloth, 4s. 6d.

———— *Little Foxes.* Cheap Edition, 1s.; Library Edition, 4s. 6d.

———— *Betty's Bright Idea.* 1s.

———— *My Wife and I; or, Harry Henderson's History.* Small post 8vo, cloth extra, 6s.*

———— *Minister's Wooing,* 5s.; Copyright Series, 1s. 6d.; cl., 2s.*

* *See also* Rose Library.

Stowe (Mrs. Beecher). Old Town Folk.   6s.; Cheap Edition, 2s. 6d.

———— *Old Town Fireside Stories.*   Cloth extra, 3s. 6d.

———— *Our Folks at Poganuc.*   10s. 6d.

———— *We and our Neighbours.*   1 vol., small post 8vo, 6s. Sequel to "My Wife and I."*

———— *Pink and White Tyranny.*   Small post 8vo, 3s. 6d.; Cheap Edition, 1s. 6d. and 2s.

———— *Queer Little People.*   1s.; cloth, 2s.

———— *Chimney Corner.*   1s.; cloth, 1s. 6d.

———— *The Pearl of Orr's Island.*   Crown 8vo, 5s.*

———— *Little Pussey Willow.*   Fcap., 2s.

———— *Woman in Sacred History.*   Illustrated with 15 Chromo-lithographs and about 200 pages of Letterpress.   Demy 4to, cloth extra, gilt edges, 25s.

Student's French Examiner.   By F. JULIEN, Author of "Petites Leçons de Conversation et de Grammaire."   Square crown 8vo, cloth, 2s.

Studies in German Literature.   By BAYARD TAYLOR.   Edited by MARIE TAYLOR.   With an Introduction by the Hon. GEORGE H. BOKER.   8vo, cloth extra, 10s. 6d.

Sullivan (A. M., M.P.).   See "New Ireland."

Sulphuric Acid (A Practical Treatise on the Manufacture of).   By A. G. and C. G. LOCK, Consulting Chemical Engineers.   With 77 Construction Plates, and other Illustrations.

Summer Holiday in Scandinavia (A).   By E. L. L. ARNOLD.   Crown 8vo, cloth extra, 10s. 6d.

Sumner (Hon. Charles).   See Life and Letters.

Surgeon's Handbook on the Treatment of Wounded in War.   By Dr. FRIEDRICH ESMARCH, Professor of Surgery in the University of Kiel, and Surgeon-General to the Prussian Army.   Translated by H. H. CLUTTON, B.A. Cantab, F.R.C.S.   Numerous Coloured Plates and Illustrations, 8vo, strongly bound in flexible leather, 1l. 8s.

TAUCHNITZ'S English Editions of German Authors.   Each volume, cloth flexible, 2s.; or sewed, 1s. 6d.   (Catalogues post free on application.)

———— *(B.) German and English Dictionary.*   Cloth, 1s. 6d.; roan, 2s,

* *See also* Rose Library.

Tauchnitz (B.). French and English. Paper, 1*s.* 6*d.*; cloth, 2*s.*; roan, 2*s.* 6*d.*

—— *Italian and English.* Paper, 1*s.* 6*d.*; cloth, 2*s.*; roan, 2*s.* 6*d.*

—— *Spanish and English.* Paper, 1*s.* 6*d.*; cloth, 2*s.*; roan, 2*s.* 6*d.*

—— *New Testament.* Cloth, 2*s.*; gilt, 2*s.* 6*d.*

Taylor (Bayard). See " Studies in German Literature."

Tennyson's May Queen. Choicely Illustrated from designs by the Hon. Mrs. BOYLE. Crown 8vo (*See* Choice Series), 2*s.* 6*d.*

Textbook (A) of Harmony. For the Use of Schools and Students. By the late CHARLES EDWARD HORSLEY. Revised for the Press by WESTLEY RICHARDS and W. H. CALCOTT. Small post 8vo, cloth extra, 3*s.* 6*d.*

Thebes, and its Five Greater Temples. See ABNEY.

Thirty Short Addresses for Family Prayers or Cottage Meetings. By "FIDELIS." Author of "Simple Preparation for the Holy Communion." Containing Addresses by the late Canon Kingsley, Rev. G. H. Wilkinson, and Dr. Vaughan. Crown 8vo, cloth extra, 5*s.*

Thomson (J.) Through Cyprus with the Camera, in the Autumn of 1878. Sixty large and very fine Permanent Photographs, illustrating the Coast and Inland Scenery of Cyprus, and the Costumes and Types of the Natives, specially taken on a journey undertaken for the purpose. By JOHN THOMSON, F.R.G.S., Author of " Illustrations of China and its People," &c. Two royal 4to volumes, cloth extra, 105*s.*

Thorne (E.) The Queen of the Colonies ; or, Queensland as I saw it. 1 vol., with Map, 6*s.*

Through the Dark Continent: The Sources of the Nile; Around the Great Lakes, and down the Congo. By HENRY M. STANLEY. 2 vols., demy 8vo, containing 150 Full-page and other Illustrations, 2 Portraits of the Author, and 10 Maps, 42*s.* Seventh Thousand. Cheaper Edition, crown 8vo, with some of the Illustrations and Maps. 1 vol., 12*s.* 6*d.*

To the Arctic Regions and Back in Six Weeks. By Captain A. W. M. CLARK KENNEDY (late of the Coldstream Guards). With Illustrations and Maps. 8vo, cloth, 15*s.*

Tour of the Prince of Wales in India. See RUSSELL.

Trees and Ferns. By F. G. HEATH. Crown 8vo, cloth, gilt edges, with numerous Illustrations, 3*s.* 6*d.*

Turkistan. Notes of a Journey in the Russian Provinces of Central Asia and the Khanates of Bokhara and Kokand. By EUGENE SCHUYLER, Late Secretary to the American Legation, St. Petersburg. Numerous Illustrations. 2 vols, 8vo, cloth extra, 5th Edition, 2*l.* 2*s.*

Two Americas ; being an Account of Sport and Travel, **with** Notes on Men and Manners in North and South America. By Sir ROSE PRICE, Bart. 8vo, with Illustrations, 2nd Edition, 18s.

Two Friends. By LUCIEN BIART, Author of "Adventures of a Young Naturalist," "My Rambles in the New World," &c. Small post 8vo, numerous Illustrations, 7s. 6d.

Two Supercargoes (The) ; or, Adventures in Savage Africa. By W. H. G. KINGSTON. Square imperial 16mo, cloth extra, 7s. 6d. Numerous Full-page Illustrations.

*U*P *and Down ; or, Fifty Years' Experiences in Australia,* California, New Zealand. India, China, and the South Pacific. Being the Life History of Capt. W. J. BARRY. Written by Himself. With several Illustrations. Crown 8vo, cloth extra, 8s. 6d.

*V*ANDENHOFF *(George, M.A.).* See "Art of Reading Aloud."

—— *Clerical Assistant.* Fcap., 3s. 6d.

—— *Ladies' Reader (The).* Fcap., 5s.

Verne. The Exploration of the World. By JULES VERNE. With 59 Illustrations by L. BENETT and P. PHILIPPOTEAUX, and 50 fac-similes of Ancient Drawings. Demy 8vo, cloth extra, 12s. 6d. ; gilt edges, 14s.

Verne's (Jules) Works. Translated from the French, with from 50 to 100 Illustrations. Each cloth extra, gilt edges—

Large post 8vo, gilt edges, price 10s. 6d. *each. Those marked* *, *in plainer binding, cloth,* 5s.

  1. *Fur Country.
  2. *Twenty Thousand Leagues under the Sea.
  3. *From the Earth to the Moon, and a Trip round It.
  4. *Michael Strogoff, the Courier of the Czar.
  5. Hector Servadac.
  6. Dick Sands, the Boy Captain.

Imperial 16mo, *gilt edges, price* 7s. 6d. *each. Those marked with* * *in plainer cloth binding,* 3s. 6d. *each.*

  1. *Five Weeks in a Balloon.
  2. *Adventures of Three Englishmen and Three Russians in South Africa.
  3. *Around the World in Eighty Days.
  4. A Floating City, and the Blockade Runners.
  5. *Dr. Ox's Experiment, Master Zacharius, A Drama in the Air, A Winter amid the Ice, &c.
  6. The Survivors of the "Chancellor."
  7. *Dropped from the Clouds.
  8. *Abandoned.
  9. *Secret of the Island.

Verne's (Jules) Works, continued :—

10. *The Child of the Cavern.
11. *The Mysterious Island. 3 vols.
12. The Begum's Fortune.
13. The Tribulations of a Chinaman.

The following Cheaper Editions are issued with a few of the Illustrations, in paper wrapper, price 1s. ; *cloth gilt,* 2s. *each.*

1. Adventures of Three Englishmen and Three Russians in South Africa.
2. Five Weeks in a Balloon.
3. A Floating City.
4. The Blockade Runners.
5. From the Earth to the Moon.
6. Around the Moon.
7. Twenty Thousand Leagues under the Sea. Vol. I.
8. —— Vol. II.   The two parts in one, cloth, gilt, 3s. 6d.
9. Around the World in Eighty Days.
10. Dr. Ox's Experiment, and Master Zacharius.
11. Martin Paz, the Indian Patriot.
12. A Winter amid the Ice.
13. The Fur Country.   Vol. I.
14. —— Vol. II.   Both parts in one, cloth gilt, 3s. 6d.
15. Survivors of the "Chancellor."   Vol. I.
16. —— Vol. II.   Both volumes in one, cloth, gilt edges, 3s. 6d.

Visit to the Court of Morocco.   By A. LEARED, Author of "Morocco and the Moors."   Map and Illustrations, 8vo, 5s.

WALLER (Rev. C. H.) The Names on the Gates of Pearl, and other Studies.   By the Rev. C. H. WALLER, M.A.   Second edition.   Crown 8vo, cloth extra, 6s.

—— *A Grammar and Analytical Vocabulary of the Words in* the Greek Testament.   Compiled from Brüder's Concordance.   For the use of Divinity Students and Greek Testament Classes.   By the Rev. C. H. WALLER, M.A.   Part I., The Grammar.   Small post 8vo, cloth, 2s. 6d.   Part II. The Vocabulary, 2s. 6d.

—— *Adoption and the Covenant.*   Some Thoughts on Confirmation.   Super-royal 16mo, cloth limp, 2s. 6d.

Wanderings in the Western Land.   By A. PENDARVES VIVIAN, M.P.   With many Illustrations from Drawings by Mr. BIERSTADT and the Author, and 3 Maps.   1 vol., demy 8vo, cloth extra, 18s.

War in Bulgaria: a Narrative of Personal Experiences.   By LIEUTENANT-GENERAL VALENTINE BAKER PASHA.   Maps and Plans of Battles.   2 vols., demy 8vo, cloth extra, 2l. 2s.

Warner (C. D.) My Summer in a Garden.   Rose Library, 1s.

Warner (C. D.) Back-log Studies. Boards, 1s. 6d.; cloth, 2s.

———— *In the Wilderness.* Rose Library, 1s.

———— *Mummies and Moslems.* 8vo, cloth, 12s.

Weaving. See "History and Principles."

Whitney (Mrs. A. D. T.) Hitherto. Small post 8vo, 3s. 6d. and 2s. 6d.

———— *Sights and Insights.* 3 vols., crown 8vo, 31s. 6d.

———— *Summer in Leslie Goldthwaite's Life.* Cloth, 3s. 6d.

Wills, A Few Hints on Proving, without Professional Assistance. By a PROBATE COURT OFFICIAL. 5th Edition, revised with Forms of Wills, Residuary Accounts, &c. Fcap. 8vo, cloth limp, 1s.

Wirt Sikes. See "British Goblins."

With Axe and Rifle on the Western Prairies. By W. H. G. KINGSTON. With numerous Illustrations, square crown 8vo, cloth extra, gilt, 7s. 6d.

Witty and Humorous Side of the English Poets (The). With a variety of Specimens arranged in Periods. By ARTHUR H. ELLIOTT. 1 vol., crown 8vo, cloth, 10s. 6d.

*Woolsey (C. D., LL.D.) Introduction to the Study of Inter-*national Law; designed as an Aid in Teaching and in Historical Studies. 5th Edition, demy 8vo, 18s.

Words of Wellington: Maxims and Opinions, Sentences and Reflections of the Great Duke, gathered from his Despatches, Letters, and Speeches (Bayard Series). 2s. 6d.

World of Comets. By A. GUILLEMIN, Author of "The Heavens." Translated and edited by JAMES GLAISHER, F.R.S. super-royal 8vo, with numerous Woodcut Illustrations, and 3 Chromo-lithographs, cloth extra, 31s. 6d.

Wreck of the Grosvenor. By W. CLARK RUSSELL. 6s. Third and Cheaper Edition.

*X*ENOPHON'S *Anabasis; or, Expedition of Cyrus.* A Literal Translation, chiefly from the Text of Dindorff, by GEORGE B. WHEELER. Books I to III. Crown 8vo, boards, 2s.

———— *Books I. to VII.* Boards, 3s. 6d.

London:

SAMPSON LOW, MARSTON, SEARLE, & RIVINGTON,

CROWN BUILDINGS, 188, FLEET STREET.

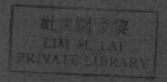